RETHINKING EROS

SEX, GENDER, AND DESIRE IN ANCIENT GREECE AND ROME

BRIAN CARMANY

authorHOUSE®

AuthorHouse™
1663 Liberty Drive
Bloomington, IN 47403
www.authorhouse.com
Phone: 1-800-839-8640

First published by AuthorHouse   11/1/2010

ISBN: 978-1-4520-9287-4 (sc)
ISBN: 978-1-4520-9288-1 (e)

Library of Congress Control Number: 2010915739

Printed in the United States of America

This book is printed on acid-free paper.

Certain stock imagery © Thinkstock.

Contents

Introduction

RETHINKING EROS USES MODERN POPULAR culture to examine sex, bodies, and gender in the ancient world in all their complexities. Three decades of Feminist and Queer Theories, Deconstruction, and the New Historicism (to name but a few disciplines) have been enlisted in the study of gender and sex in Antiquity with profitable results. As a contribution to the ongoing discourse, the present study will use contemporary popular culture to examine ancient texts. Operating under the working assumption that popular culture is "good to think with," we will along the way have a little help from friends as diverse as Bill Clinton and Paris Hilton.

Although neither of us realized it at the time, my belief in the ability of popular culture to illuminate widespread cultural constructions dates back to 1997, when my mother and I had a weekday ritual of watching the afternoon lineup of small claims court TV shows (*Judge Judy, The People's Court,* and *The Divorce Court* when summer vacations allowed). Although I was fifteen years old and not yet aware of Marxist criticism, I intuitively knew on some level that these televised spectacles were culturally-encoded masquerades of class and gender parading as informed legal proceedings.

To the best of my knowledge, popular culture has yet to be utilized in a full-length study of classical Antiquity, and it is this lack which the present book aims to fill. To provide an overview of the pages to come, the first two chapters read ancient texts and modern scholarship alongside *The Starr Report*. *The Starr Report* is Kenneth W. Starr's documentation for his recommendation to impeach President William Jefferson Clinton. Being a collection of gossip, testimony, email, etc. culled from diverse sources and presented to an eagerly-awaiting public, *The Starr Report* offers readers a highly fictionalized account of the Monica Lewinsky-Bill Clinton "scandal." Much of the Report's testimony is of questionable legal relevance; more important is it's value as a cultural document indicative of gender roles and public interest.

Chapter three compares ancient Roman satire of Jews and Ethiopians in light of email jokelists regarding Mattel Barbie dolls. The bodies of Jews and Ethiopians fascinated Roman writers to no end. More specifically, the barbarian penis was the subject of endless jokes, both visual and written. Much as the gendered bodies of barbarian "others" generated numerous jokes, the overly feminized body of Mattel's fashion icon has been the source of much contemporary humor.

The fourth chapter brings the still emerging discipline of porn studies to examine the books of Ezekiel and Hosea. A number of biblical scholars are beginning to note the pornographic content of certain sections of these books. There has, however, yet to be a serious attempt to grapple with the relevance or appropriateness of using pornography as a heuristic framework for studying of biblical texts. Given the dizzying amount of pornography available in a number of mediums, to focus my study I made the rather arbitrary choice of surveying celebrity sex tapes. I did so under the assumption that it is the protagonists involved that ensured these work's popularity. Celebrity sex tapes make for poor quality porn, and Ezekiel 16 hardly ranks as a work of great literature. As a cultural historian I read biblical texts and porn as documents like any other; those who insist on doing otherwise will find little solace in these pages.

Chapter five juxtaposes occurrences of pirates in the ancient Greek novel with contemporary mass market women's romantic fiction (most commonly known as "Harlequin Romances," much as the facial tissue is called the "Kleenex," and sometimes as "bodice rippers" owing to their covers). As well will see, pirate abductions of beautiful heroines form a sub-genre of the historical romance, with interesting parallels to the depiction of pirates in the ancient novella.

Be it foolishness or wishful thinking, I hope that this work will be of interest to the general reader or student of contemporary culture as well as the specialist. To aid in this regard, I have tried my best to avoid esoteric shorthand familiar to the classicist but unknown outside the field. As familiar letters are more readable and accents a hindrance, I have transliterated all Greek letters. Translations of Sappho, the Greek novella, and the Pseudpigrapha are from Harris, Reardon, and Charlesworth respectively; all others are from the Loeb Classical Library unless otherwise noted. I make no claims to literary eloquence, and my own translations veer towards the literal. The studies in this book are linked thematically, and can be safely skipped over according to the reader's interests without any great loss in argumentation.

I never anticipated being referred to by colleagues as a "sexologist" or (more amusingly) "sexpert." Since, however, the label seems to have stuck, I would like to offer a note regarding the present work's subject matter and style. The time for Victorian euphemisms and quaint sexual-anatomical circumlocutions is over. In response to the not inconsiderable number of kind reviewers who found this book's frank discussions sordid or unnecessary, I can only counter that I believe honest reflection makes it self-evident that a squeamish reluctance to approach sexuality in our primary texts in a forthright manner amounts to intellectual dishonesty. As a cultural historian, I believe we do our primary sources the greatest courtesy to treat biblical texts and porn (a multi-billion dollar industry and here to stay) as documents like any other. Those who insist otherwise will find little solace in these pages.

As *The Starr Report* exists in a number of editions and media, page numbers have been omitted; for the reader's convenience I have given the Barbie lore variants discussed in Thomas (2003). Appendixes tangential but relevant to the subjects at hand have been added as back matter. The final two chapters are hopefully readable, but perhaps of less interest to the non-specialist. Chapter six traces the history of women's bodies in classical science, and concludes with the surprising afterlife of ancient medical discourse, namely it's serving as the direct impetus behind today's masturbatory female vibrators. Chapter seven uses semiotic theory in an exegesis of Judges 3, arguing for homoerotic connotations in Eglon's meeting with Ehud. Understanding that semiotic theory hardly makes for light reading, I take two well-known children's books -Lewis Carroll's *Alice Through the Looking Glass* and Roald Dahl's *The BFG*- as points of inspiration for illuminating our discussion.

A number of friends and colleagues have taken the time out of their busy schedules to read portions of these chapters throughout their gestations, and it gives me great pleasure to offer my deepest gratitude to the following for their thoughtful criticism: Victor Gould, Claudia Graziano, Mia Park, Jean-Francois Racine, Judy Yates Siker, Justin Smith, Ken Stone, Mary Ann Tolbert, and Seung Ai Yang. Finally, special thanks are due to my family -Christy, David, Diana, Laura, and Mark- who, although they might wish I spent less time playing with Barbie dolls and watching porn, have provided me with unflagging support, critical feedback, and love.

ONE

Sappho in the Oval Office

This chapter will explore the ways in which two women have been overly determined in the public eye so as to make their stories nearly unintelligible. Separated by millennia, Monica Lewinsky and Sappho might seem an unlikely choice for comparison. However, as we shall see presently, the poetess and former White House Intern have more in common than one might think. Their gender and sexuality have cast spells powerful enough to obscure their words and stories.

Indeed, Sappho has been so overly-sexualized that scholars have emended fragment 99 to include the word *olisbos* –dildo – when five of the seven letters are uncertain, and two missing: "the occurrence of the word *olisbos* here is far from certain; every letter of olisb- is printed in the Greek editions with a dot underneath, a convention used be editors of papyri to indicate the uncertainty of decipherment. The Sapphic dildo may be a figment of papyrological imagination" (Snyder 115).

Sappho's gender has also led to conceptions of her poems as artless, psychological outpourings of her inner emotional life (see Lefkowitz1996: 26 for critique). Fragment 94, for instance, has found little adoration:

tethnakén d' adolós theló
a me psisdomena katelimpane
oim(oi) os deina peponthamen....
chairoisa ercheo k' amethen
memnais'....
oistha gar ós se pedepoman
ai de me alla s' ego thelo
omnaisai....

"I ......really wish I were dead."
She, shedding many tears, was leaving me
and she said to me:

"Oh my! What awful things we have had to endure,
Psappho. It is really unwillingly that I leave you now...."

And I answered her with these words:
"Go away in happiness, remembering
Me, for you know how I cared for you.

And if you don't know, I want to
Remind you......... (if)
and we felt lovely things..."

Bowra's interpretation, for instance, borders on the biographical: "[here] Sappho looks back on times which they have passed together, and enumerates activities which must have been the common round of their lives....The simplicity of her manner has some of the qualities of the conversation which she claims to record, and it is hard not to believe that such conversation took place" (1962: 192). Even less charitably, Denys Page reduced the poem to a "long list of girlish pleasures" (1955:83). Had Sappho been male, Page might have noticed the beautifully interwoven multiplicity of voices existing simultaneously in fragment 94, or appreciated its tightly-knit structure.

To offer one more example, consider fragment 31, Sappho's famous *phainetai moi* poem:

phainetai moi kénos isos theoisi
emmen' ónér , ottis enantios toi
isdanei kai plasion ádu phóneisas
upakouei
kai gelaisas imeroen, to m' é eptoaisen
ós gar es se idó broche', ós me phónais'
oud en et' eikei
alla kam men glóssa m' eage, lepton
d' autika chró púr upadedroméken
oppatessi d' ouden en orémmi, epirrhombbeise
d' akouai
kad de m' idrós kakcheetai, tromos de
paisan agrei, chlórotera poias
emmi, tethnakén d' oligó 'pideués
phainom' em' auta

He appears to me like unto the gods,
That man, who opposite to you
Sits and to you speaking a sweet word,
he replies,
to your lovely laughter. Truly that
Flutters my heart in my breast.
For when I look at you for a moment,
I can not speak
But my tongue is broken, right then
Over my skin a light fire races,
I see nothing with my eyes, my ears
Rumble,
And sweat pours over me a trembling
Seizes me entire, greener than grass
I am, just about to die
I seem to me.

George Devereux -and he is not alone in this interpretation- opines that we find in Fragment 31 a highly neurotic lesbian suffering from a female castration complex: "The core of the problem can best be stated in somewhat colloquial terms: 'What does this man – and indeed any man – have that Sappho does not have?' 'What can a man offer to a girl that Sappho cannot offer?' The answer, I think, is obvious and leads to a clinically highly documentable and crucial finding: few women are as obsessed with a (neurotic) feeling of incompleteness with the clinically commonplace 'female castration complex' – as the masculine lesbian. Moreover, the latter experiences her 'defect' with violent and crushing intensity…" (1967: 22).

GIRL-TALK WITH THE TATTLETALE INTERN

More recently, Lewinsky's has suffered similar obfuscations. In 1998 the public eagerly awaited Kenneth Starr's voluminous document outlying the grounds for impeaching then-President Bill Clinton. The finished product known as *The Starr Report* (actually a compilation of many interviews, sworn testimonies, e-mails, transcripts of illegally recorded telephone calls, subpoenaed objects, etc.) was, in the words of Fedwa Malti-Douglas, a "highly gendered narrative parading also as a legal text" (2000: x).

Simply put: Lewinsky talked too much throughout her testimony, which made her easy to depict and deride as a flighty Chatty Cathy. And of course Kenneth Starr was there to dutifully record every emotional outburst, "um," poor attempt at demonstrating proficiency in French, and nervous giggle. Whereas Clinton held his own throughout the investigation, responded with succinct answers, and proffered the response "I'm going to revert to my former statement" with unflagging predictability. Lewinsky, on the other hand, "complies energetically with the investigators' requests for copious of the pedestrian movements and mundane details of personal lives. She takes seriously – and proceeds as though the investigators are inquiring in good faith…" (St. John 2004: 33).

The Report exploits every opportunity to capitalize on Lewinsky's loquacious testimony, bringing us into feminized realms of gossip and intrigue of questionable legal relevance, such as Lewinsky's Harlequin romance-inspired fantasies (i.e. "I don't care what you say, but if you were 100% fulfilled in your marriage I never would have seen that raw, intense sexuality that I saw a few times – watching your mouth on my breast or looking in your eyes while you explored the depth of my sex"). The text lays excessive emphasis on Lewinsky's obsession with being thin ("I didn't keep this dress as a souvenir. I was going to wear it on Thanksgiving and my cousins, who I always try to look skinny for because they're all so skinny..."). As Maria St. John wryly notes: "Lewinsky is not a feminist performance artist, but throughout her testimony she performs American femininity in ways that exceed even the masculinist demands of the moment of confession she inhabits" (2004: 33). At times Monica is described as "peevish," "very emotional," "aggressive," "ma[king] a stink," and "known as the stalker among her peers."

The *Report* lays great stress on her zeal for the "18 or so" gifts the President gave her, which casts Lewinsky in the light of a gift-grabbing materialist: "In early September, Ms. Currie gave several Black Dog items to Ms. Lewinsky. In an email message to Catherine Davis, Ms. Lewinsky wrote 'Well, I found out from Betty yesterday that he not only brought me a t-shirt, he got me 2 t-shirts, a hat and a dress!!!!'" Monica is also overly-feminized through the "Narrative's" insistence to keep her in a dress, although this is perhaps due to her own preoccupation with the garment:

Q: Now directing your attention back to February 28th, -- 1997, the day that you wore the blue cocktail dress --
A: It's not a cocktail dress.
Q: Okay, I'm sorry.
A: No, that's Okay. I'm a little defensive about this subject. I'm sorry.
Q: How would you describe the dress?
A: It's a dress from the Gap. It's a work dress. It's a casual dress.
Q: With respect to that dress...
A: Right, I'm sorry.
Q: ... you mentioned that you believe that there could be semen on it. Could you describe what you did with the President that led you to believe that?

A: We were in the bathroom and -- can I close my eyes so I don't have to...

Q: Well, you have to speak up. That's the only...

Lewinsky and Sappho on Male Inadequacy

These examples of ways in which Sappho and Lewinsky's gender and sexuality have been overly-determined by editors, writers, and scholars are telling in their persistency. One topic, however, that commentators have been more reticent to discuss is even more revelatory in its silence. In the public's zeal for penetrative cigars, voyeuristic masturbation, and breath mints, a much more interesting discourse has gone largely unnoticed: the President's apparent inability to bring Lewinsky to climax. One searches the Starr Report in vain for evidence of Clinton-induced orgasms. As the "Narrative" would have it, Monica's personal sexual gratification would seem to lie in her ability to make the President come: "And I continued to perform oral sex and then he pushed me away, kind of as he always did before he came, and then I stopped and said...I care about you so much;...I don't understand why you won't let me...make you come; it's important to me; I mean, it just doesn't feel complete, it doesn't seem right."

By any reasonable standards, Clinton's sexual prowess left something to be desired. Curiously, the media paid scant attention to the President's less-than-virile body. When elaborating upon their lack of genital-genital contact, Monica testified that "their genitals only briefly touched: 'We sort of had tried to do that, but because he's so tall and he couldn't bend because of his knee, it didn't really work.'" Elsewhere the reader is told that "During many of their sexual encounters, the President stood leaning against the doorway of the bathroom across from the study, which, he told Ms. Lewinsky, eased his sore back." Furthermore, once during phone sex late one night "the President fell asleep mid-conversation."

In conclusion, given the parallel Sappho-Starr Report trajectories we have already traced, it is perhaps no surprise that generations of scholars managed to read gay sex and lesbian dildos into unintelligible Sapphic fragments while overlooking male sexual inadequacy in fragment 105a:

> *Oion to glukumalon ereuthetai akroi ep usdoi,*
> *akron ep akrotatoi, lelathonto de maladropes*
> *Ou man eklathont, all ouk edunant epikesthai*
> "she (is) like ----- the sugar-apple that grows red on the high branch,
> high on the highest one, but the apply pickers missed it.
> Oh no, they did not miss it, they were not able to reach it...."

In fragment 105a, a bridal song, the *melon* fruit signifies both woman and clitoris. Customarily translated as "apple," *melon* is a general word for fleshy fruit and various clitoral objects (Winkler 1990: 183). Here the fruit *ereutho* - "blushes," or "reddens" (flushes with blood/heat) yet lies out of the (masc.) apple-picker's reach. Whereas scholars have been overly ingenious in locating phantom dildos, Sappho's critique of male sexuality has yet to be fully explored.

Two

WORD PLAY WITH THE PRESIDENT

LEXICOGRAPHY, THE ART OF DEFINING words and task of many a classicist, seldom makes for exciting reading. It was quite a coup, then, for Bill Clinton to manage to make wordplay interesting. Even more impressive is that fact that it was the third singular of the most common verb in the world that made international headlines: "It depends what the meaning of 'is' is." As observed by Sasha Torres, there existed considerable moral anxiety about Clinton's sexual pedantry, "which emerges from the language of the definition itself, and from legal language generally....namely, *that words sometimes mean more than one thing*, even within a single sentence" (2001: 106 her emphasis).

Clinton's remark was variously perceived as being lawyerly jargon at best, a form of guilt at worst, or −most accurately- a masterstroke of rhetoric. In the sentence "It depends on what the meaning of the word 'is' is", the word "is" functions as both noun and verb. The ambiguity provided "the decision to strategically stabilize the meanings of words –constitutes the linguistic positivism of legal discourse, a positivism that Clinton here simultaneously undermines and exploits" (Torres 2001: 106).

Although another statement received less attention, more remarkable still (and inspiring for scholars hoping to get their work published and read) is this bit of wordplay:

> According to what the President testified was his understanding, this definition "covers contact by the person being deposed with the enumerated areas, if the contact is done with an intent to arouse or gratify," but it does not cover oral sex performed on the person being deposed; he testified:
>
>> "If the deponent is the person who has oral sex performed on him, then the contact is with -- not with anything on that list, but with the lips of another person. It seems to be self-evident that that's what it is. . . . Let me remind you, sir, I read this carefully."
>
>> In the President's view, "any person, reasonable person" would recognize that oral sex performed on the deponent falls outside the definition.

As if working wonders with the verb "to be" was not extraordinary enough, here Clinton manages to turn the word "if" into a tour de force of pedantry that is indeed self-evidently factual. The obsessive need for Kenneth Starr and his aides to pinpoint the definition of what actually constitutes sex brought about the confusion itself. One of the many conflicting and convoluted definitions of sex that their pretense of scholarly rigor was the following three-part definition of "sexual relations" in Clinton's January 17 deposition:

> "For the purposes of this deposition, a person engages in sexual relations when the person knowingly engages in or causes:
>
> 1. Contact with the genitalia, anus, groin, breast, inner thigh, or buttocks

of any person with an intent to arouse or gratify the sexual desire of any person;

2. Contact between any part of the person's body or an object and the genitals or anus of another person; or

3. Contact between the genitals or anus of the person and any part of another person's body.

Contact means intentional touching, either directly or through clothing."

The public was equally eager to discuss the vagaries of sex acts (perhaps most famously, Oprah opined that oral sex does in fact constitute sexual relations). To aid in this regard, newscasters threw their own wrenches into the socket, like the absurd lack of clarity in Larry King and Bob Woodward's CNN coverage on the grand jury tapes of 21 September:

Woodward: You and I were talking about the definition that the president…

King: He has the actual three-part definition…

Woodward: that the president was given in his Paula Jones deposition. It's so technical, but essentially the first part of it says "was there contact with the privates?"

King: Mention them all?

Woodward: and it lists six areas, we'll call them the big six. And in…

King: Item out.

Woodward: And that they allowed in and it doesn't include oral sex. When you look at the definition number three which says contact between the privates and any other part of the body.

King: So the judge in throwing out two and three – this is the deposition throws out contact between any person's body and an object, et cetera, or another. You think that he was technically correct in saying – in concept, to the one thing she left in, I did not have sex?

Although I suffer no delusions of grandeur that my own attempt at lexicography will set the nation aflame, I would like to explore the meaning of a rare Greek word, *arsenokoites*, approaching the term via a collection of noncanonical Jewish writings known as the Sibylline Oracles. Scholars are as obsessed with the word as the public was with "is" during the Clinton impeachment proceedings, and oceans of ink have been spilt in debates over its precise meaning. There is good reason for doing so: the word has been translated as "homosexual" in the Second Testament (1 Cor. 6:9, 1 Tim 1:10), providing ammunition for homophobic fools of various stripes. By juxtaposing this stab at word-definition alongside presidential wordplay, we will find a number of illuminating parallels between ancient polemic and the sexual invective surrounding the Clinton-Lewinsky "scandal." It is of course necessary to approach the subject in light of its cultural context, which I have provided in Appendix Three for those unacquainted with homoeroticism in the Ancient Near East.

HOMOEROTICISM IN THE SIBYLLINE ORACLES

The collection of Jewish and Christian writings known as the "Sibylline Oracles" were compiled between the second century B.C.E. and the sixth century C.E. Dating the various works is problematic. It is possible, however, to discern actual historical events in the oracles which helps fix approximate dates to the texts (see, for example, the eruption of Vesuvius in 79 C.E. described in 4.130 and the reference made to the emperor Hadrian in 5.48). Collections of Sibylline oracles enjoyed considerable popularity among Gentiles long before Jews and Christians made use of them. The sibyl was an inspired prophetess who could impart wisdom to humans, "making known to them the will of the gods and showing them what course to take in any great emergency" (Torrey 1945: 108).

Sibyls were celebrated in numerous places, from Babylonia to Italy. The Sibyl became connected with the famous Greek shrine at Delphi, where her oracles were preserved in hexameter verse; she later became connected with Cumae in Italy. Ovid describes the Sibyl as a haggard ancient virgin (already 700 years old and destined to live another 300 years) who declined Apollo's offers of marriage and immortality: "eternal, endless life was offered me, had my virgin modesty consented to Phoebus' love....The time will come when length of days will shrivel me from my full form to but a tiny thing, and my limbs, consumed by age, will shrink to a feather's weight" (*Metamorphoses* 6.130). Plutarch describes the Sibyl's speech as visceral prophecy spoken through frenzied lips: "uttering words mirthless, unembellished, unperfumed, yet reaches to a thousand years with her voice through the god" (*Moralia* 397a).

The Sibylline Oracles played an important role in Greco-Roman Antiquity. Dionysius of Halicarnassus writes that the oracles were highly prized by the Romans and played a crucial role in their political life: "There is no possession of the Romans, sacred or profane, which they guard so carefully as they do the Sibylline oracles. They consult them, by order of the senate, when the state is in the grip of party strife or some great important prodigies and apparitions have been seen which are difficult of interpretation" (*Roman Antiquities* 6.62). Suetonius records how Augustus formed a collection of oracles and deposited them in the temple of Apollo (*Aug.* 31.1).

The Jews began to make use of the Sibyl for their own propaganda: "Beginning with a strong nucleus of pagan oracles, it was possible through interpolation and gradual expansion to introduce monotheism, the Mosaic ordinances, and important features of the Hebrew history to mankind" (Torrey 1945: 109). The similarity of Hellenistic oracles to Old Testament prophecies against foreign nations made for an easy appropriation of the format. The Sibyl's pagan identity lent the weight of authority - readers were getting information about Jewish history and moral concerns through an impartial outside observer.

A similar strategy lies behind the *Starr Report*'s presentation of data, gossip, and minutiae. The *Report* goes to great pains to seem as impartial and authoritative as possible, as clearly seen by its length, organization, needless detail, recycled information, and some 1,500 footnotes. The document opens with a list of chronologically ordered "Key Dates" spanning November 1992 and September 9 1998, continuing with a "Table of Names," "Narrative," "Acts that May Constitute Grounds for Impeachment", "Notes," and a "Conclusion." The first two sections can be immediately dismissed as wholly irrelevant, mainly serving the purpose of seeming officious (the "Key Dates" end with the submission of the Referral to Congress "pursuant to 28 U.S.C. 595 (c)," and the "Table of Names" lists 153 individuals subdivided into "The Principals," "Lawyers and Judges," "Monica Lewinsky's Friends/Family/ Acquaintances"). The following three sections –"Narrative," "Acts," Notes"- rehash the same material but are loaded with needless citations and typeset so as to seem equally impressive. The "Conclusion" serves no purpose, consisting of one sentence "This Referral is respectfully submitted on the Ninth day of September, 1998 Kenneth Starr, Independent Counsel."

Another strong resemblance between the *Report* and the Oracles is the specter of (im)morality, poorly disguised as legal infraction in the former, explicit in the later. While the sin of adultery lurks throughout the Report, one of the most pronounced functions of the Jewish-Christian Sibylline Oracles is moral exhortation - of which sexual impropriety plays a leading role. The oracles follow a pattern wherein destruction is a punishment for sins and can be avoided by morally-upright behavior. Although numerous forms of injustice, violence, and sexual offenses are condemned in the Sibylline Oracles, male-male sexual acts feature especially prominently. Indeed, the Sibylline Oracles make more frequent use of homosexual perversion as a sign of deviance from God than any other contemporary Jewish-Christian writings.

As with other noncanonical texts, it is often difficult to determine the extent to which homoerotic behavior is connoted in many passages in the Sibylline Oracles. A representative verse is 4.34: "Neither have they disgraceful desire for another's spouse or for hateful and repulsive abuse of a male." Similarly, the extent to which the sin of Sodom is to be read as one of homosexual perversion is ambiguous. Another representative verse: "For you alone, land of Sodom, evil afflictions are in store" (6.21). The oracles themselves never connect Sodom with homosexuality and - as noted in the appendix - a Jewish connection between Sodom and homoeroticism in Antiquity is tenuous.

A similar ambiguity exists in many of Clinton and Lewinsky's liaisons. As Dana Nelson and Tyler Curtain note, "something about the Clinton-Lewinsky relationship is definitely queer: in fact, nearly all of the dense meanings and confluence of representations that are said to constitute 'homosexuality' circulate within this only nominally heterosexual relationship....[Monica's] navy blue dress from the Gap was stained on a day that included the bestowal of a copy of Walt Whitman's Leaves of Grass...and a rim job by Monica Lewinsky on William Jefferson Clinton... Whitman has been used as a shibboleth for nonnormative sexuality since his first writings, and rimming is the religious right's new "unspeakable" crime: it's a new sodomy" (2001: 41).

And then of course there is the famous cigar, which defied even the *Starr Report*'s obsessive taxonomies and inspired considerable amateur Freudian psychoanalysis. Phrases like "At one point, the President inserted a cigar into Ms. Lewinsky's vagina" float throughout the text, disembodied from any semblance of relevancy to the topics at hand. Only once does the Report add that afterwards the President "then put the cigar in his mouth and said 'It tastes good.'" The cigar figures prominently in an early encounter wherein "she and the President moved to the Oval Office and talked. According to

Ms. Lewinsky: 'He was chewing on a cigar. And then he had the cigar in his hand and he was kind of looking at the cigar in…sort of a naughty way. And so…I looked at the cigar and I looked at him and I said, we can do that, too, some time.'"

If queerness remains latent in the Report, the oracles at times condemn homoerotic practices in clearer form, and it is to these condemnations that we now turn a Kenneth Starresque eye in an attempt to classify, scrutinize, and define forms of "sexual relations." Many passages in the oracles condemn male same-sex practices in clearer form. In keeping with their Greco-Roman background, most passages denounce pederasty specifically, although a few condemnations of general male homoeroticism are to be found. Determining what specific form of homoeroticism is under discussion is often a matter of scholarly debate. A catalogue of vices preserved in Book 2, for example, contains a prohibition against *arsenokoitia* literally "the bedding of males"), a problematic word of uncertain meaning: "Do not steal seeds. Whoever takes for himself is accursed to generations of generations, to the scattering of life. *mē arsenokoitein*, do not betray information, do not murder" (2.71-73).

As previously mentioned, the meaning *arsenokoitia* of has been much debated in recent scholarship. Due to its appearance in the vice catalogues of 1 Cor. 6:9 and 1 Tim. 1:10, the term has received ample consideration from biblical scholars, with little agreement. Among the most influential writers, on the assumption that sexual acts in Antiquity were motivated primarily by commerce or economic greed, John Boswell argued that *arsenokoites* referred to male prostitution (1980: 344) and William Countryman suggested that it described "legacy hunters who used sexual attraction as bait" (1988: 128). Neither Bowell nor Countryman, however, cite any source which employs the term in a way that supports their hypotheses.

David Wright has suggested that the term was coined from the Septuagint translation of Lev. 18:22 and 20:13 (1984: 126). Wright's following argument asserts that since Lev. 18:22 and 20:13 make no grammatical reference to children, the term denounced all forms of male homoeroticism. I find Wright's etymology unconvincing; in any case, however, even if Wright is correct, the fact that all Hellenistic Jewish writers interpreted Lev. 18:22 and 20:13 in terms of pederasty supports my own hypothesis. More recently Dale Martin has also argued that *arsenokoites* was not a simple reference to homosexual sex. (1996: 121-2). Martin's suggestion, however, rests on the unsubstantiated claim that the arrangements of sins in a vice list can shed light on their meaning. Neither biblical nor extra-biblical catalogues of vices show any tendency to categorize their contents.

I will here put forth the argument that *mē arsenokoitein* should here be rendered "do not practice pederasty." A survey of primary sources reveals that all but one of the term's occurrences which allow us to decipher its meaning describe pederasty. Two early sources explicitly link *arsenokoitia* with pederastic abduction; both works portray Zeus as the archetype of the lustful pederast. Aristides' *Apology* makes one of the earliest references to the term. Chapter 9 of the *Apology* describes Zeus' many mortal lovers. Verses 8-9 tell of Zeus' sexual relation with Ganymede, the young handsome shepherd. Later, in chapter 13:7, Aristides refers back to the act as a sign that the gods committed *arsenokoitia*.

In a second work, Hippolytus's *Refutation of all Heresies*, Zeus is again described as a pederast. Hippolytus (170-236 C.E.) tells a Naassene Gnostic myth about the seduction of Adam and Eve by the evil being Naas. In passage 5.21.22-23 Hippolytus tells us that Naas first committed adultery with Eve. Naas then went to Adam and "possessed him like a boy". This is how adultery and *arsenokoitia* came into the world. Hippolytus writes that Zeus was Naas and Ganymede was Adam (5.21.35).

In his *Preparation for the Gospel* 6.10.25.3 the church historian Eusebius (260-340 C.E.) quotes the Syriac writer Bardesanes (154-222 C.E.): "From the Euphrates river all the way to the ocean in the East, a man who is derided as a murderer or a thief will not be the least bit angry; but if he is derided as an *arsenokoites*, he will defend himself to the point of murder" (trans. by Martin 123). To Bardesanes' original statement Eusebius adds his own additional comment: "Among the Greeks, wise men who have *erōmenous echontēs* are not condemned" (trans. by Martin 123). Here the diminutive term *erōmenous echontēs* "little darlings", "little beloveds" allow us to identify this occurrence as another reference to pederasty.

In the sixth century chronicles of John Malalas we again find an equation of *arsenokoitia* with pederasty. Malalas writes that the Byzantine emperor Justinian (527-65 C.E.) castrated bishops who committed *paiderastia*, *androkoitēs*, and *arsenokoitia*: "In that year some of the bishops from various provinces were accused of living immorally in matters of the flesh and of *arsenokoitoutes*....The emperor immediately decreed that those detected in *paiderastia* should have their genitals amputated" (*Chronographia* 18.166-168).

One remaining pre-Byzantine source employs the word to describe anal intercourse between husband and wife; the author of a Greek penitential falsely attributed to John the Faster (d. 595 C.E.) apparently understood *arsenokoitia* to refer to anal intercourse that could occur heterosexually. After listing various forms of incest the author writes, "In fact, many men even commit the sin of *arsenokoitia* with their wives." (trans. by Wright 139). The final occurrence of the term (of questionable value because of its late date but still worth mentioning) is another explicit description of pederasty found in the twelfth century *Scholia in Aristophanes, scholia in plutum*. With numerous formulaic expressions of grief, verse 153.5 bemoans the morally substandard habits of *arsenokoitai* who are amorous of boys and make them lawful.

The word *koitē* - "bed" - appears again in 5.386 with clearer grammatical sense of "the bedding of boys": "Matricides, desist from boldness and evil daring, you who formerly impiously catered for pederasty (*oi to palai paidōn koitēn eporizet' anagnōs*).

3.185-6 describes both pederasty and intercourse between adult males:

"Male will have intercourse with male and they will set up boys in houses of ill-fame (*arsēn d' arseni plēsiasei stesousi te paidas aischrois en tegeessi*).

In regards to the intercourse between adults, neither *arsēn* nor *arseni* are diminutives - these are not male children. *Plesiasei*, of *plesiazō* is rare in Jewish-Christian writings but common enough in Classical Greek. In its primary sense the verb means "to be near, in proximity to" (LSJ 1420). Derived meanings can include "consort, associate with" and "have sexual intercourse with" (LSJ 1420). The sexual meaning given in Collin's translation "have intercourse with" is sufficiently attested in ancient texts (Demosthenes *Speeches* 40.8 - marital infidelity; Hyperides 1.3 - a bride on her wedding night; Isocrates *Letters* 3.36 - sexual relations between husband and wife).

Pederasty is also referenced in 3.186 with the setting up of boys in "houses of ill-fame", *aischrois en tegeessi*, literally "shameful roofs". This is a description of the prostitution of boys. In later Greek *tegeessi - tegos* developed a specialized meaning of "brothel or stew" (LSJ 1765).

Another reference to pederasty is found in 3.596: "and they do not engage in impious intercourse with male children" (*kou de pros arsenikous paidas mignuntai anagnos*). As with the previously discussed *plēsiasei*, *mignuntai* and cognates appear infrequently in Jewish literature but are well attested in the works of Gentile writers. Homer and Pindar both employ the term to describe illicit sexual unions (*Iliad* 9.275, *Pythian Odes* 3.14). The word also appears to have had more specific connotations of incest, with Sophocles twice using the word to describe Oedipus' incestuous relations with his mother (*Oedipus Tyrannus* 791, 995); Aristophanes also employs the word to describe incest, here between brother and sister (*Frogs* 1081). The adjective used to describe the pederastic relations (*anagnos* of *anagneia*, "abominable, wickedness, unpurified, unclean, unholy, defiled" LSJ 101) alerts us to an important value judgment being made on the coupling, connecting the vice with filth and impurity.

A related adjective, *asthesmos*, is used to describe pederasty in 5.166: "With you are found adulteries and illicit intercourse with boys" (*moicheiai para soi kai paidōn mixis athesmos*). Here pederastic relations are paired with *moicheia*, adultery. Although *mixis* ("intercourse with others, especially sexual intercourse or commerce" LSJ 1136) is not a common verb in Hellenistic Jewish writings, the adjective *asthesmos* occurs with some frequency in Jewish texts (3 Maccabees 5:12, 6:26 - Ptolemy's lawless plan to execute the Jews; Josephus *War* 7.264 - unlawful food; 2 Peter 3:17 - lawless persons, probably Gentiles; Sib. Or. 5.177 - unspecified lawless persons who will inhabit the lawless nether region of Hades). The adjective is always employed pejoratively, meaning "unprincipled, unseemly, disgraceful, lawless" (BDAG 24).

Of special note here is an occurrence of *asthesmos* in the New Testament with a possible (dubious, I'd argue) connotation of homoeroticism: "and if he rescued Lot, a righteous man greatly distressed by the licentiousness (*aselgeia*) of the lawless (*ton asthesmōn*) - for that righteous man, living among them day after day, was tormented in his righteous soul by their lawless deeds that he saw and heard" (2 Peter 2:7-8 NRSV). Again, the extent to which the sin of Sodom was to be understood as one of homosexuality is unclear. Licentiousness (*aselgeia*) occurs frequently in the New Testament and first Century Jewish writings with no usual connotation of homoeroticism (BDAG 141).

Asthesmos appears once again in 5.430, another condemnation of pederasty: "No adulteries or illicit love of boys" (*ou de yamoxlopiai kai paidōn Kurpis athesmos*).

Again pederastic relations are paired with adultery (in this case *gamochlopiai*). Here the expression "illicit love of boys" (*paidōn Kurpis athesmos*) makes use of Cyprus, a name for Aphrodite used in the abstract for "love or passion" (LSJ 1012).

Conclusion

In sum, then, the Sibylline Oracles devote considerable attention to the denouncement of male same-sex practices, usually pederasty. In the oracles the vice serves as a tool to illustrate Gentile depravity while highlighting the righteousness of Torah-observant Jews. Of course the obvious point of comparison here is the use of the Republican Party's predictable use of the Clinton impeachment hearings as a crisis of morals. The condemnations of sexual practices found in these texts are both exceptional and unremarkable. No other Jewish-Christian text devotes so much attention to homoeroticism or makes such extensive use of venomous language in its description of the vice, and arguably no other case of adultery has evoked such media attention. The uniformly negative attitudes towards homoeroticism and adultery found, however, are entirely congruent with general Judeo-Christian attitudes on the subjects.

Three

Barbie among the Ancient Romans

The bodies of certain "Others" were of great interest to the Romans, perhaps especially those of Jews and Ethiopians. Depictions of Jews in Roman satire share much in common with caricatures of Ethiopians in Roman bath mosaics in that both forms of representation focus on their subjects' penises *ad naseum*. These outlets for humor, then, offer the historian an invaluable window into configurations of desire and fear of the sexualized body. As we will see, Barbie also provides the cultural critic with a number of lenses which help to make sense of these representations. If Mattel's iconic wonder-doll is good for anything (and she is), it is parody of class, gender, race, and sexuality. Thus I will enlist Barbie in my exploration of the meanings that these verbal and pictorial jokes carry.

Satire is a genre of literature that humorously ridicules foolish or senseless behavior. The satirist's chief aim is to expose vices or stupidity that his audience should avoid. A satirist's weapons are irony, witticisms, and poetic exaggeration. Although humorous in nature, the primary goal of satire is not to provoke laughter. Instead, satire aims to school its audience in proper modes of behavior by criticizing prevalent vices and follies that ought be avoided. By ridiculing fruitless beliefs and actions, more appropriate ways of life are shown by comparison.

Satirical references to Judaism can only be understood in the context of ancient humor. Like all forms of Roman comedy, satire made use of stock characters. Roman satire occasionally made reference to specific Jews, but more often poked fun at fictitious stereotypes. Such casual over-simplifications of Jewish characters must not be viewed as particularly venomous attacks on Judaism. The satirical use of common types was instead so widespread as to be expected.

Roman satire did not employ abstract speculation or highly theoretical musing. It focused instead on the everyday, common aspects of society. It is for this reason that Jewish bodies drew more attention from satirists than did differences in the Jew's unique religious beliefs, diet, poverty, and Sabbath leisure. Depictions of the Jews in ancient Roman satire were formulaic in that they shared a number of common themes. These oft-recurring and overlapping themes include: circumcision; abstention from pork; Jewish poverty; Sabbath leisure; and Jewish licentiousness (see Appendix Two for a survey of primary sources).

Judging from our extant sources, Romans had a seemingly obsessive fascination with the Jewish penis. Circumcision is by far the most prevalent theme in ancient references to Judaism; indeed, the custom is mentioned in most satirical depictions (see Juvenal *Satires* 14.104; Martial *Epigrams* 7.30, 7.82, 11.94; Persius *Satires* 5.184; Petronius Fragment 37. As Steve Mason notes, "the Jews were so closely associated with the practice that they could be referred to simply as 'the circumcised' without further qualification" (1990: 150). Circumcision was an affront to Roman tradition and aesthetics. Greco-

Roman art celebrated the foreskin in precise detail as an emblem of masculine beauty. Removal of the foreskin was viewed as an immoral act of mutilation; circumcision was thus a visible sign of barbarian deviance.

The purpose of satire is to ridicule bizarre practices; Roman identity was reinforced by mocking the wayward habits of deviants. It is therefore not surprising that ancient satire made extensive use of circumcision as a clear sign of Jewish perversion. For the satirist, "the circumcised" was an decidedly pejorative term. The custom could be derided and then ignored with no further explanation.

And so we have the words of Petronius (died *ca.* 65 CE), who jokes about his dutiful slave: "He has only two faults, and if he were rid of them he would be simply perfect. He is circumcised and he snores" (*Satyricon* 68.8). Petronius is able to criticize his slave for being circumcised without justification. His audience would have understood the insult and agreed with his conclusion. In other words, circumcision was so grotesque that its' foolishness was evident and did not need to be expounded on.

Jewish males were frequently depicted as making good use of their considerable endowments, especially by Martial. This stereotypic description of the lascivious, sexually potent Jew was a common Roman attack on barbarians, who were thought to lack the moral fortitude needed to abstain from pleasure. The Jew's considerable sexual potency was evidenced by their large genitals. Martial refers to the unsuccessful attempts of a Jewish actor to hide his unusually big penis with a large sheath (7.82). After likening his own genitalia with that of his slave, Martial proudly announces them both to be befitting of a Jew (7.35). When his friend Chrestus, a pathic, offers to fellate the poet, Martial suggests that he instead search for a Jewish partner (7.55); the Jew's prodigious member will test Chrestus' skills at fellatio.

Jewish lasciviousness is a cause of frequent jealously for Martial. He vents his anger at a Jewish poet who seduced his favorite boy (11.94). The Jew not only rivals Martial in poetry but in courtship. He elsewhere ponders why a woman, Caelia, prefers Jews to Romans:

> You grant your favours to Parthians, you grant them to Germans...; and for you from his Egyptian city comes sailing the gallant of Memphis, and the black Indian from the Red Sea; nor do you shun the lecheries of circumcised Jews.... What is your reason that, although you are a Roman girl, no Roman lewdness has attention for you? *Epigrams* 7.30.

The themes here are ones of sexual jealousy; what most galls the poet is that her lovers all belong to foreign nations. Martial is reflecting a fear that foreigners can replace (or even worse be preferred to) Roman men.

Barbie's Fantastical Plasticity

Barbie serves children and adults alike a number of purposes, more than Mattel could have imagined when she debuted in February 1959. According to the company's canonical spin, Mattel co-founder Ruth Handler came up with the idea when observing her own daughter, Barbara (Barbie's purported namesake), playing with paper dolls. Handler, so the story goes, wanted to take this play-time to the next dimension, and the rest -as they say- was history. This quaint tale of attentive motherhood is at odds with a better-documented version involving Lilli - a German doll designed not to appeal to children, rather "sold to adult men in tobacconists and bars. [She] came in one of two sexy outfits, and if there was an aura of fantasy at all around this doll, it was an adult male's pet" (Schneider 1987: 26) - serving as the prototype, but no matter.

The facts of Barbie's biography are these: née "Barbie Millicent Roberts", an early novel, *Barbie's Fashion Success*, informs us that she moved to the town of Willows (located in the unspecified nowhereville of the Midwest) just before starting high school due to her father - a naval pilot- got a job transfer (Rand 1995: 52). Her previous origins are unknown, as is the explanation of her father's odd naval deployment to the Midwest. Further information is scant. In terms of family we know only that she is the daughter of George and Margaret, and cousin to one Lulu Belle Rawlins from New Orleans. In Barbie's *New York Summer* we hear her lament being "sixteen going on seventeen," fretting over whether her ponytail is too childish for her age (Rand 1995: 52). In 1961 Barbie got a boyfriend, Ken, followed by a friend, Midge, in 1963. Quickly realizing that much of Barbie's appeal lies in her consumer's ability to project her into any given fantasy, Mattel soon backpedaled, and after the early 1960's we learn nothing more about her.

Like many Barbie researchers, I was astonished at how eager people were to share their recollections and opinions on this eleven-and-a-half inch girl wonder. This eagerness to talk about Barbie is reflected by the innumerable (and often hilarious) jokes, lists, and "e-lore" in circulation that parody her (Thomas 2003: 158). Barbie is no stranger to pranks. In the early 1990's a group calling itself the Barbie Liberation Organization (BLO) exchanged Barbie and G.I. Joe's talking mechanism in several popular toy stores, the effect being that Barbie would bark "Vengeance is mine!" and "Eat lead, Cobra!" while Joe would exclaim "Let's go shopping!" and "Will we ever have enough clothes?" (Thomas 2003: 118).

Barbie's fortieth birthday occasioned many e-mail forwards still crossing the paths of cyber-space (her fiftieth birthday seems to have drawn less attention; more on this later). Making the rounds under a number of titles, lists of fictitious "new" Barbie's were much discussed. A popular version included:

> **Bifocals Barbie. Comes with her own set of blended-lens fashion frames in six wild colors (half-frames too!), neck chain and large-print editions of *Vogue* and *Martha Stewart Living*.
> **Hot Flash Barbie. Press Barbie's bellybutton and watch her face turn beet red while tiny drops of perspiration appear on her forehead! With hand-held fan and tiny tissues.
> **Facial Hair Barbie. As Barbie's hormone levels shift, see her whiskers grow! Available with teensy tweezers and magnifying mirror.
> **Cook's Arms Barbie. Hide Barbie's droopy triceps with these new, roomier-

sleeved gowns. Good news on the tummy front too: muu-muus are back! Cellulite cream and loofah sponge optional....

The dolls promoted in this spoof press-release most obviously address anxiety of the discontents of aging. Below the surface, however, runs an interesting discourse on the de-sexualized body, with frank humor serving as commentary on the mundane, (societally deemed) unattractive features (flabby arms, female facial hair, sweaty brow) which the Mattel doll markedly/marketably fails to represent.

A variant lists in alphabetical order "Barbie's We'd Like to See" and is worth quoting at length:

Admin Barbie: Works twenty-hour days for little pay (80 percent of Admin Ken's salary) and is the lowest on the totem pole despite being the one that actually runs the group. Comes with mini-laptop. Pull the string on her back and she'll schedule a meeting with your other dolls, replace the toner cartridge in the laser printer, coordinate a re-org and a move, and order airline tickets for Director Ken....
Bag Lady Barbie: Complete with shopping cart; wearing everything she owns.
Barbie Bobbit: With knife, Ken had better watch out.
Barbie Brown Simpson: Slashed neck and bloody body, carton of Ben & Jerry's Cookie Dough included.
Battered Wife Barbie: Comes with a restraining order to serve Ken.
Birkenstock Barbie: Finally, a Barbie doll with horizontal feet and comfortable sandals. Made from recycled materials.
Bisexual Barbie: Comes in a package with Skipper and Ken.
Black Barbie: Once your Ken doll goes black, he'll never go back.
Blue-Collar Barbie: Comes with overalls, protective goggles, lunch pail, UAW membership, pamphlet on union-organizing and pay scales for women as compared to men. Waitressing outfits and cashier's aprons may be purchased separately for Barbies who are holding down second jobs in order to make ends meet.
Boulevard Barbie: With cheap makeup, short skirt, and high heels.
Bow-wow Barbie: The ugliest Barbie you've ever seen.
Breast Implant Barbie: Now Barbie's a D-cup.
Brunette Barbie: The only Barbie with a brain.
Bulimorexia Barbie: Also no different in appearance from regular Barbie.
Cancer Patient Barbie: Remove the wig and Barbie's bald.
Crack Addict Barbie: Pipe included, sugar may be used to simulate crack-

cocaine.

Dinner-Roll Barbie: A Barbie with multiple love handles, double chin, a real curvy belly, and voluminous thighs to show girls that voluptuousness is also beautiful. Comes with a miniature basket of dinner rolls, Bucket O' Fried Chicken, tiny Entenmann's walnut ring, a brick of Sealtest ice cream, three packs of potato chips, a t-shirt reading "Only the Weak Don't Eat," and, of course, an appetite....

Feminist Barbie: Has unshaved legs and armpits.

Homegirl Barbie: Truly fly Barbie in midriff-bearing [sic] shirt and baggy jeans. Comes with gold jewelry, hip-hop accessories, and plenty of attitude. Pull cord and she says things like "I don't think so," "Dang, get outta my face," and "You go, girl." Teaches girls not to take shit from men and condescending White people.

Lesbian Barbie: Barbie with a butch.

Lipstick Lesbian Barbie: Actually no different in appearance from regular Barbie.

Melrose Place Barbie: Comes complete with her Barbie Dream Apartment, where Skipper and the rest live rent-free. Other accessories include a bottle of vodka, silk sheets, and an arrest warrant.

Mobile Home Park Barbie: Comes complete with hair in rollers and pregnant. Accessories include two toddlers. When you pull the string on her back she asks where her gov't support check is. Some Mobile Home Barbies come with surprise Ken or G.I. Joe since they often give her surprise visits when they come into town.

Murder, Barbie Wrote: Whenever this elder stateswoman of the Barbie-set (she's twenty-seven!) arrives in the playhouse, all the other dolls mysteriously disappear.

My So-Called Barbie: She faces the same troubling issues as regular teens who don't have huge wardrobes, perfect bods, pools, and ponies.

Navy Pilot Barbie: Comes with a body bag, wrecked fighter jet sold separately.

Oprah Barbie: Push a button on her back and this Barbie actually speaks! Hold your very own talk show with topics like how tough math class is, Ballerina Barbie's struggle with bulimia, Kens who wear Barbie's clothes.

Our Barbies Ourselves: Anatomically correct Barbie, both inside and out, comes with spreadable legs, her own speculum, magnifying glass, and detailed diagrams of female anatomy so that little girls can learn about their bodies in a friendly, non-threatening way. Also included: tiny Kotex, booklets on sexual responsibility. Accessories such as contraceptives, sex toys, expanding uterus with fetus at various stages of development, and breastpump are all optional, underscoring that each young woman has the right to choose what she does with her own Barbie.

Punk Barbie: Has rings in all sorts of places.

Quantum Physicist Barbie: Yeah, right.

Rabbi Barbie: So, why not? Women rabbis are on the cutting edge in Judaism. Rabbi Barbie comes with tiny satin yarmulke, prayer shawl, teffilin, silver kaddish cup, Torah scrolls. Optional: tiny mezuzah for doorway of Barbie Townhouse....

It is unlikely that Mattel envisioned welfare checks, contraceptives, clit rings, Torah scrolls, or breastpumps entering the collective Barbie fantasy; equally improbable is the chance that the company will acknowledge in its PR literature the fact that most products on this wish-list do more to address the socio-economic realities of women in a gender stratified capitalistic society than the canonical toy does herself. Unfortunately space does not permit the full analysis this piece of e-lore deserves. Happily, a narrower focus on the function of bodily humor in the list still proves instructive, especially in regards to the text's foregrounding of Barbie's physical inaccuracies. Recent estimates put the possibility of having a body shaped like Barbie's is less than one hundred thousand; luckily the change of having Ken's physique is one in fifty (Thomas 2003: 119). In foregrounding the discrepancy between image and reality, the folklore gives expression to a shared discourse on the here problematical female form; clearly Barbie is "good to think with."

HYPERSEXUALIZED BLACK MEN

These preoccupations -ancient and modern- with Jewish male bodies and plastic females have a direct analogue with the frequent depictions of perpetually erect, well-endowed black African men, and spoof "ethnic" Barbies. These images of Africans became a staple in bath-house architectural decoration throughout the Roman Empire. Among the most common type of representations are painted scenes of black pygmies cavorting on the banks of the Nile. Usually executed with great skill, such renderings give the impression that sub-Saharan African life was a gas for all. Consider, for instance, the merry outdoor banquet fresco excavated at Pompeii, House VIII (ca. 45-79 C.E.); the drinking party, comically huge phalluses, and (heterosexual) couplings stand in stark contrast with the awkward-looking crocodile busy devouring a pygmy (now at the Naples Archaeological Museum, inv. 113196). The attentive detail given to the sumptuous couches, pleasure barges, and drapery effectively highlight the atmosphere of hedonism.

Although a number of mosaics depicting servile black bath attendants are closer to economic realities, the subjects' hyperbolic penises are no less fanciful than the Nilotic scenes (see among others the floors of Pompeii, House of the Menander [I,10,4] and House of Caesius Blandus [VII, 1, 40] - both *in situ*, *ca.* 40-20 B.C.E.). An attendant from a pavement at Timgad possesses what might be the largest member given to a mortal in classical Antiquity, a prick that even the satyrs might envy! Further emphasizing his sexual prowess is the impressive stream of ejaculatory fluid threatening to flood the ground beneath him (the grip of his left hand leads me to believe that he is masturbating, not urinating - although the possibility cannot be ruled out). Not quite as macrophalic but even happier is a carefree male servant prancing above a free-floating, disembodied vaginal shape complete with clitoris (House of the Menander [I, 10, 4]).

Enter Barbie once more to our discussion. We have already met ebonics-savvy "Homegirl" Barbie; she had some twenty-five years to build up her street cred, getting her first black friend in 1968 (Rand 1995: 68). Although black and Hispanic Barbies appeared in 1980, Mattel again backpedaled, deciding that dolls of color could no longer claim the Barbie name. To split the difference, 1991 introduced three new black fashion dolls: Shani, Asha, and Nichelle (their relation to Barbie is unclear). It takes little effort to discern the latent blackploitation behind Matel's press releases, which invariably describe Shani products as "outrageous," "ethnic," "exotic," or garbed in "shimmering ethnic print":

> SHANI is tomorrow's African-American woman. She's young, strong, beautiful, and fresh, She exemplifies every attribute insinuated by her Swahili name, which translates as "MARVELOUS"....SHANI knows what she wants and has the self-confidence to go after it being the best she can be. SHANI is fun, but she is also serious. Not "just a pretty face," she has high aspirations for

her future. She's also very conscious of her culture, which she views as a rich tapestry of history, culture, and family values. With a look that moves easily across the terrains of West Africa to sunny horizons of the Caribbean and on to the cosmopolitan metropolis' [sic] of America, SHANI is equally at home in kente cloth or glittering glamour... (Mattel Information Release cited in Rand 1995: 68).

I find myself uncertain what to make of Barbie's "ethnic" and "outrageous" friends. Contemporary folklore, however, finds Mattel's marketing gimmicks equally disconcerting and hilarious. One of my favorite pieces of cyber-lore is the line of "Indian Barbie Dolls:"

Commod Barbie: comes with, can opener and cheese slicer added bonus, she comes with pliers and thread to make a jingle dress out of commod lids (available at Cree reservations only!)....
"49" Barbie: sits in her pick-up til her beer is gone, then closes in on next snag, come sunlight she's gone
Chorus Girl Barbie: sits in her lawn chair, making fun of all the dancers, but when her drum gets the song, she stands up to sing and all the men really dance their best....
Wannabee Barbie: jet black (Clairol) hair, brown cordoury dress, made in japan mocs and beadwork, turkey feather fan and an attitude that is intolerable.
Non Indian Mam Married to an Indian Barbie: attends every meeting and ceremony and uses terms like "we" and "us", often times feels compelled to speak out, as in "what Mr. so and so really means is, blah, blah, blah....
New Age Barbie: comes with her own crystals, beads and "sacred" smudge shell....
"My Great Grandmother Was Cherokee" Barbie: exact replica of regular Barbie, no distinction from every other Barbie in store....

Such texts offer commentary on Mattel's failure to convey the rich complexities of their product's (purported) cultures. In this regard Barbie provides a striking parallel to the aforementioned Roman mosaics and frescos. What these representations have in common is a stubborn reluctance to show the bodies of ethnic "Others" in their full complexity. The strategy, rather, is to reduce overly-racialized bodies to commoditized penises and breasts of sizes ranging from the improbable to the impossible.

Moving Towards a Deeper Understanding of Humor

What, ultimately, are we to make of these images? Is a joke merely a joke? Is a toy ever simple child's play? The answers are both affirmative and negative. On one hand, distinctive Jewish characteristics were not ridiculed more frequently or vehemently than any other unusual practices. The Greeks, for example, fair far worse in Juvenal's satires than do the Jews. Satire seeks out peculiar or unseemly habits in order to illustrate how one should not live. It is therefore to be expected that Jewish oddities were targeted by satirists. Since all strange customs were laughed at, such joking does not indicate an exceptional anti-Jewish bias. Similarly, black Africans are not laughed at than any other barbarian ethnic group. But does this mean that there is nothing of significance here? People do not express ideas purposelessly, so why were these sentiments being expressed? Barbie might be the bane of numerous feminists, but judging from the fact that Mattel has sold billions (yes, billions) of dollars worth of dolls, clearly the majority of mothers are sufficiently nonplused.

Humor and art employ a wide variety of ideals, prejudices, and jibes that are made meaningful through culturally shared beliefs that either implicitly or explicitly contrast how one ought to act with how some people are thought to act. So what made these anti-Jewish and Ethiopian jokes meaningful? I believe that the answer lies in the issues of group identity; the satirists attacked these foreigners because they perceived their otherness to be a threat to Roman identity. Although voiced in a variety of forms, Roman humor invariably provides "a furious attack on the foreigners who have poured into Rome from Greece and the Near East to ruin its society and its morals" (Highet 1962: 68). I am not arguing that all ancients shared an extreme hatred of Jews and Africans; such a conclusion poses problems of both logic and evidence. Humor carries a poetic license to exaggerate and run to extremes. The Jews were discussed in a number of ways in antiquity, and many sympathies towards the religion have been documented. Ancient literary texts betray more geographical ignorance than racial prejudice against blacks. What I suggesting -and what Barbie has helped me to realize- is that these jibes are indicative of a loose prejudice that found ready markets both Roman and globally capitalist.

FOUR

Ezekiel the Pornographer?
Getting Hardcore with the Prophets

Ezekiel 16 is a condemnation of the people of Jerusalem, who are described as idolaters who broke their covenant with Yahweh. Drawing parallels between marriage and covenant, Jerusalem is depicted as a faithless whore who defiles her privileged relationship with the deity. Ezekiel employs the metaphor of prostitution to promote his monotheistic agenda. The harlot's insatiable appetite for new flesh is meant to mirror the Israelite's lust for numerous deities. This paper will explore Ezekiel's metaphor of adultery in chapter 16, a troubling text which raises a number of problems for exegetes. Mary Shields explains that:

> By any account, Ezekiel 16 is a problematic passage and the most extreme case among the prophetic oracles of accusation that use marital and sexual imagery....The problems begin with the Hebrew language. Virtually all the English

translations of this passage gloss over and tone down the ways in which body parts are named. They also subdue the violence of the imagery (1998: 5-6).

In Ezekiel 16, Jerusalem is abandoned by her birth parents and then reared by Yahweh. Verses 1-7 portray Jerusalem as a child of humble origins: she is a foreigner (Canaanite, Amorite, and Hittite 16:3) whose birth occasioned no ceremonial rites or pampering (16:4). Instead of receiving paternal or maternal care the child was rejected and left to lie in her own blood (16:5). The repeated description of Jerusalem's blood (birth blood, menstrual blood, and the hymenal blood associated with her marriage to Yahweh) emphasizes her body's uncleanliness: "the only time the woman is clean in this passage is when Yahweh washes and clothes her. By repeatedly connecting women with uncleanness, the text places women completely outside the boundaries of society" (Shields 1998: 13).

Yahweh bestows no affection on the girl and expresses little concern for her until she reaches sexual maturity: "Not interested in the asexual child... he takes notice of her again only when she is sexually mature and ready for intercourse" (Day 2000: 208). From the onset the woman is both sexualized and objectified: the male deity and author(s) characterize the woman through her female form. Jerusalem's body is exposed to the male gaze. The audience is invited to share Yahweh's pleasure in the woman's firm breasts, pubic hair, and nakedness (16:7). Jerusalem's naked body (emphasized by two terms for nakedness - "You were naked and bare" 16: 7) is offered for the delight of the deity and Ezekiel's audience; both deity and reader also share a voyeuristic pleasure in the repeated formula "I passed by you and saw" (16:6, 8).

Yahweh quickly penetrates the woman (16:8). The expression "I spread My robe over you" (16:8) is a euphemism for sexual and marital relations (see Ruth 3:9). One can also not help but wonder if the thrust of the preceding marriage formula "I *entered* into a covenant with you" (16:8) is also meant to be evocative of sexual penetration. In any case, Yahweh's mention of the children born to him by Jerusalem (16: 20-21) make it clear that sexual intercourse occurred between husband and wife.

Yahweh then lavishes costly gifts on his new bride, verses 10-13 portraying him as a doting husband. Jerusalem is treated like royalty (16:13). She eats only the best foods (16:13) and is adorned with expensive jewelry and precious cloth (16:10-13). It is Yahweh who clothes and adorns Jerusalem's body; she is an object to be acted upon. Mary Shields explains that "the only beauty the woman has is not her own, but rather, the beauty of her adornments, which reflect her husband's power and honor" (1998: 10). That Jerusalem's beauty derives from Yahweh is emphasized in 16:14: "Your beauty won you fame among the nations, for it was perfected through splendor which I set upon you."

Their marriage soon gets messy. Jerusalem's fame spreads among the nations (16:14) until she grows so confident in her beauty that she plays the harlot (16:15). The verb used here, *znh*, means in its most basic sense to "commit fornication" (BDB 275). The Hebrew term for "prostitute", *zona*, is essentially "a professional or habitual fornicator, a promiscuous or unchaste woman, whose role and profession are defined by her sexual activity with men to whom she is not married" (Bird 1989:78). In the Hebrew Bible the verb is largely limited to women and is used to describe a wide number of illicit sex acts with no necessary reference to an economic exchange for sexual favors.

Jerusalem's sins in Ezekiel 16 indicate the multivalent nature of *znh*; indeed, her sexual indiscretions seem to know no bounds. Ungrateful Jerusalem uses the expensive cloth that Yahweh had given to her to construct platforms on which to fornicate (16:16). She gives Yahweh's choice foods to her lovers (16:19) and sacrifices her children to them (16:20-21). The woman then begins to attract an international crowd, indiscriminately spreading her legs to all her neighbors (16:25-29).

The text is explicit: "the erotic imagery and vocabulary scandalize, bordering on the pornographic" (Day 2000: 205). Day's statement begs the question, in what ways can the text be meaningfully described as pornographic? At a larger level, to what extent can pornography (and porn studies) be used as a heuristic device in the study of ancient works? Some etymologizing might prove useful here. The component of the Greek word *pornographos* can be discerned easily enough - *porne* (whores), *graphe* (depictions) -depictions of whores. So far so good. What we find in Hosea (see below) and Ezekiel 16 are at their most basic level literary representations of whoring women.

A surface level analysis of a word's component roots, however, fails to address the complexities and technologies of porn in the twenty-first Century. In this regard, Andrea Dworkin takes the etymology surprisingly literally: "Contemporary pornography strictly and literally conforms to the word's root meaning: the graphic depiction of vile whores, or, in our language, sluts, cows (as in: sexual cattle, sexual chattel), cunts. The word has not changed its meaning and the genre is not misnamed" (1981: 200). In a different vein, Susanne Kappeler focuses on the viewer of the discourse rather than the representation itself: "pornography, like much other public imaging, is constructed for male viewing," creating the male as subject and the female as object (1986: 32, 51-53). T. Dorah Setel has also offered several explanations as to why pornography is created. Setel has suggested that pornography: serves as tangible proof of male superiority; satisfies a psychological need for a sense of power; and arises in response to any change in the power relationship between women and men which increases the autonomy of women (1985: 88).

Even a cursory glance at Ezekiel 16 shows that Setel's first two suggestions are indeed correct. The language and imagery of Ezekiel 16 undeniably legitimates male authority and empowers its intended male audience. Setel's third suggestion, that pornography arises in response to changes in the patriarchal system which lessen male authority, is perhaps substantiated by the role of prostitutes in the Greco-Roman world. Although the role of prostitutes in ancient Israelite society is ambiguous, "it has been suggested that they constituted an established urban group outside of the unity of family and household, and by implication, the system of marriage and female control" (Setel 1985: 89).

In an age where a bewildering number of sexually explicit images are readily available through print, video, web, etc., the once helpful distinction between hardcore and softcore pornography is beginning to outlive its usefulness, and one is hard pressed to find contemporary pornography analogous to the imagery found in Ezekiel and Hosea's sustained narratives of adultery. As we shall see presently, however, I have found that the sub-genre of celebrity sex tapes offers several illuminating points of comparison that warrant discussion and help us to understand the workings of pornographic imagery in literary texts. Although I have neither the time nor space (nor bandwidth) to fully engage with the sub-gene in detail, I have chosen one example owing to its marked similarity in narrative technique. The differences, however, are equally telling; most notably, Pamela Anderson and Tommy Lee's couplings are touching in their mutuality.

Of the porn surveyed, *1 Night in Paris* (distributed by Red Light District and starring hotel-heiress Paris Hilton and her lesser known then-boyfriend Rick Salomon) most closely approximates our biblical texts in terms of narrative. These are demonstrably male fantasies. Rick provides the film's only narrative framework by introducing each scene with telling commentary. The film opens with a fully clothed Rick chewing gum, unsuccessfully affecting an air of ease and familiarity with the viewer: "Hey I'm Rick, and this is my one night in Paris. Check it out!" Rick straightaway addresses the film's poor quality, explaining that "this is night vision which is now black and white -there's no more green in it. uh. I think it looks pretty cool its my favorite part of the movie this black and white, I think it's the most hardcore, fun, it looks like we're having a good time...."

It is no coincidence that Rick's favorite footage is a close-up of him masturbating, for the entire film is quite masturbatory on his part. Paris' name might be assigned the title role, but there is no mistaking that Rick is the protagonist of this tale. The number of close-ups on Rick's penis is surprising -even by porn standards- and he often brings attention to the organ verbally, such as when he asks Paris (and the viewer) "Do I have the hottest dick in the world or what? wow. wow." As both narrator and performer, Rick calls the shots, constructing a web of fantasy in his positioning of Paris and gratuitous mentions of her "barely legal" age (her pigtails don't help in that regard).

It is this phallocentric shaping of narrative that brings us back to Ezekiel 16, which is constructed through similar I-you language wherein the reader only hears Yahweh's speech. This formula effectively mutes the woman. Yahweh's comment that after her punishment Jerusalem will be too ashamed to speak (16:63) is puzzling, since she never speaks in this text; the expression "open your mouth" might be a vulgar reference to Jerusalem opening her "mouth" to her lovers for sexual penetration. Jerusalem is her husband's property - bound, silenced and acted upon. Ezekiel 16 emphasizes the woman's objectification and lack of a self: "Women are completely circumscribed by this text: they are unclean and therefore unholy; their bodies and their sexuality are to be for one man alone; they are bound and covered possessions with no freedom of movement, no speech, no power....Throughout this text, power resides in one person: Yahweh" (Shield 1998: 13-14).

It is important to bear in mind that Ezekiel's metaphor of prostitution is indeed a metaphor. Peggy L. Day has astutely noted that: "metaphors do not equate one thing with another in a point-by point correspondence. Indeed, metaphors presuppose dissonance" (2000: 290-91). If a metaphor is used literally then it ceases to be a metaphor. That Jerusalem is not an actual prostitute is made explicit in the text itself: "Yet you were not like a prostitute, for you spurned fees....Gifts are made to all prostitutes, but you made gifts to all your lovers, and bribed them to come to you from every quarter for your harlotries" (16:31, 33). The text does not condemn Jerusalem for literal adultery but rather uses harlotry as a metaphor for the Israelites' polytheism.

Ezekiel 16 also draws on the metaphor of Yahweh's marriage to the Israelites. Elaine Adler has shown that in the Hebrew Bible "marriage and adultery provide the most apt metaphors for covenant and apostasy. This is suggested by the fact that many more continuous verses in the prophetic books are devoted to depicting YHWH's 'marriage' to Israel than to any of the other personal metaphors" (1989: 380). The marriage metaphor served as an effective rhetorical tool because "both marriage and YHWH's bond with Israel are relationships marked by different stages. This phasic nature of male-female relationships - which could include youthful romance, courtship, marriage, the honeymoon, betrayal, divorce and reconciliation - helps to explain the elaborate development of the marriage metaphor by Hosea, Jeremiah, and Ezekiel" (1989: 383). Adler finds it likely that when marriage was used as a symbol for Israel's covenantal relationship with the deity, a number of "associated commonplaces" would have been evoked in Ezekiel's audience: "both are relationships between unequals, with the stronger, dominant party responsible for the protection and maintenance of the other" (1989: 26).

Ezekiel falls into the prophetic tradition which makes extensive use of the marriage and prostitution metaphors. I would now like to briefly survey the metaphor of prostitution in the book of Hosea, a text which markedly shares a number of similarities with Ezekiel 16. The book of Hosea describes the people of Israel as wayward children who abandoned proper forms of worship and strayed from the true path (11:1-2). Yahweh, a dutiful parent, provided Israel with love and food (11:4), but these acts of kindness were not reciprocated. Instead of worshiping Yahweh exclusively, the people of Israel forsook their parent and worshiped other deities.

In the first chapter Yahweh commands Hosea to marry a prostitute so that he might live out the sins of Israel symbolically: "Go, get yourself a wife of whoredom and children of whoredom; for the land will stray from following the Lord" (1:2). Like the city of Jerusalem in Ezekiel 16, Hosea's wife Gomer is used as a representation of Israelite apostasy. Again, this is *metaphorical* prostitution: Gomer is characterized as a prostitute "because of her adulterous and idolatrous behavior, not because she may or may not have been a prostitute" (Setel 1985: 91).

Hosea and Gomer's marriage is a parody of the marriage of Baal and Asherah, with the three sons who are born from this union being symbolic of Israel's apostasy (1:6-8). Hosea obeys Yahweh's order, and buys himself a prostitute who bestows her affection on many men just like the Israelites bestow their affection on many gods: "Go, befriend a woman who, while befriended by a companion, consorts with others, just as the Lord befriends the Israelites, but they turn to other gods" (3:1).

The mention of the bride price (3:2) is significant. The prostitute is now Hosea's legal possession, and he can do with her as he pleases. He can now *enforce* chastity, by keeping her at home and restraining her from courting other men and other deities. Hosea informs his wife of her obligatory celibacy in terms that parallel her illegitimate behavior with the cultic transgressions of Israel: "You are to go a long time without either fornicating or marrying; even I shall not cohabit with you. For the Israelites shall go a long time without officials, without sacrifice, and without cult pillars, and without ephod and terraphim" (3:3-4).

The metaphor of marriage can be applied to the Israelites because their covenant relationship with Yahweh confers onto them a similar intimacy. The Israelite's unfaithfulness to Yahweh is described in explicit metaphors of sexual infidelity: "Wine and new wine destroy the minds of my people: It consults its stick [i.e. its phallus], Its rod directs it! A lecherous impulse has made them go wrong, and they have strayed from submission to their God" (4:11-12). In this passage spiritual and carnal fornication have become inseparably entangled.

Chapter 8 continues the metaphor of marital unfaithfulness and makes reference to how the Israelites breached their privileged union with their God: "Because they have transgressed My covenant, and been faithless to My teaching….Of their silver and gold, they have made themselves images to their own undoing" (8:1-4). The idols made from silver and gold in verse four are most likely images of Baal. A degree of irony is inherent in the passage, since the precious metals used to craft the images came ultimately from Yahweh (2:10).

How can Hosea's use of the prostitution metaphor inform our understanding of Ezekiel 16? In both texts spiritual and carnal fornication are intertwined. The Israelite's predilection for numerous gods is reflected in their cravings for multiple lovers; their sins in worship are mirrored by their lustful earthly transgressions. In both texts sin is connected with female sexuality. "'Bad' women are promiscuous and rapacious, and female desire is consuming and dangerous....Male control, then, is seen as necessary and desirable" (Exum 1996: 114).

Hosea and Ezekiel both make extensive use of metals and foreign idols to describe the habits of adulterous wives. The previously discussed Hosea 8:4, for instance, describes how the Israelites have crafted idols of foreign deities from silver and gold which came from Yahweh. Similarly, Ezekiel 16:17 describes how Jerusalem melts down jewelry given to her by Yahweh and recasts the metal into dildos (literally "male images") which she masturbates with. Note the anxiety expressed in 16:17 over the artificial penis - a fear of autonomous female sexuality which dares to operate outside the realm of the male-wielded phallus.

However, the most illuminating point of connection between the book of Hosea and Ezekiel 16 is the language of possession which both texts share. In both texts Yahweh has authority over Israel just as a husband has control over his wife. By this comparison men are likened to Yahweh and women to earthly matters. Setel explains how this dichotomy represents a view of "human males as being analogous to Yahweh, while women are comparable to the people, who, by definition, are subservient to Yahweh's will. In a dualistic division between the divine (spiritual) and human (material) spheres of existence, men are categorized as belonging to the former, while women are assigned to the latter" (Setel: 1985: 92).

The language of possession employed by Ezekiel is just one of the many problems raised by the text. Linda Day has expertly identified a number of troubling issues with Ezekiel 16 that raise problems for its interpreters. Firstly, this is unquestionably a one-sided account. Jerusalem is silenced: "nowhere are her thoughts or actions represented, except through his voice; all is seen only through YHWH's eyes" (Day 2000: 206). Secondarily, the marriage between God and Jerusalem is not consensual: "no response is required or desired on her part. *He* spreads his skirt over her, *he* covers her nakedness, *he* swears to her, *he* enters into covenant with her. Ironically, YHWH later accuses Jerusalem of breaking the oath and covenant, neglecting the fact that she never made one; she was just taken" (Day 2000: 208, emphases in original).

The depiction of Yahweh in this narrative is also difficult grapple with. He is portrayed in several unflattering ways, being overly lustful (16:8) and possessive of his bride (16:17-19). But above all else the deity's unabashed misogyny and horrific treatment of his wife are most troubling in the punishment scene (16:37-43). The reader is forced to accept Yahweh's treatment of his wife, since to question the deity would be tantamount to challenging his divine authority. The structure of the text, then, keeps the reader from questioning male dominance and sexual assault.

These problems are very real and cannot be explained away. We can, however, at least account for their presence in the narrative. Peggy Day explains that the graphic and sustained depiction of a naked female body engaged in illicit sexual acts is calculated to have an emotive effect on its male audience, both titillating them with visions of sexual activity and rousing them to righteous fury and indignation. The subject position of the now cuckolded husband functions as a powerful tool for further solidifying a united male point of view....Ezekiel 16 uses the emotionally loaded language of illicit sexuality and carnal betrayal to manipulate its audience into taking its proffered ideological position of giving cult to gods other than Yahweh and on political alliances with foreign nations (2000: 235).

S. Tamar Kamionkowski has convincingly argued that the author of Ezekiel 16, feeling disempowered by the Babylonian exile, betrays an anxiety about gender roles in his writing. "This gender ambiguity is expressed through the marital metaphor which provides the writer with an arena to explore this ambiguity in a subtle, cloaked manner" (2003: 152). The text, Kamionkowski explains, is an exploration of gender reversals.

Jerusalem's sin is that she is crossing gender boundaries and attempting to pass for an aggressive and independent male - a privilege which the narrator emphatically denies her: "In other words, Ezekiel constructs a metaphor whereby the Judean/exilic male community poses as a female (personified Jerusalem) who in turn passes for a male (independent and aggressive)" (Kamionkowski 2003: 7). The venomous and scurrilous language against Jerusalem in Ezekiel 16, then, is not only directed against women but is in fact also directed inwards. Ezekiel's diatribe against the prostitute provides him with a vehicle through which he can berate his own male community, shamming them to reform by likening them to a scandalous, unclean woman.

FIVE

SWASHBUCKLING PIRATES AND THEIR PLUNDER

PIRATES FIGURE PROMINENTLY IN THE romance novel genre. Both ancient Greek and contemporary American romance novels (most widely known as "Bodice Rippers" or "Harlequin Romances" owing to the genre's most popular publisher) make frequent reference to pirates, often with telling similarities and differences. The ancient Greek romance is primarily attested by five complete works dating from ca. 100 B.C.E. to ca. 400 C.E. (Longus's *Daphis and Chloe*, Tatius's *Leucippe and Clitophon*, Heliodorus's *Ethiopian Tale*, Chariton's *Chaereas and Callirhoe*, and Heliodorus's *Ethiopian Tale*). Numerous additional fragments dating as early as the fourth century B.C.E. attest to the genre's longstanding popularity.

Pirates serve a number of functions in the ancient novella. These ne'er-do-wells must be read alongside the considerable number of brigands and vagrants which populate the novels and serve to complicate their protagonist's reconciliations. Lowly-born pirates also serve as foils to the protagonist's aristocratic status. As Witmarsh astutely notes, the novels can: "glide easily between different temporal and spatial settings, adopting multiple perspectives upon the way. This facility allows for a larger social canvas, encompassing beggars, bandits, nurses, prostitutes, fishermen, slaves and slavers, pirates, traders, and more... it is rare to find any challenge to the truisms that bandits and pirates are bad, slaves are deceitful and manipulative, nurses are untrustworthy." (2008: 84-85).

To focus our discussion, in the pages that follow, I will read the ancient romance genre alongside two representative modern counterparts, namely Betina M. Krahn's *Passion's Ransom* and Jennifer Horsman's *Magic Embrace*, both published by Zebra Books.

Passion's Ransom
Captive Beauty.
Blythe Woolrich was a proper and respectable female. Genteelly poor and thoroughly modest, she was not at all the sort of woman to be held for ransom by a horde of nefarious pirates. And certainly not the sort whose passions could be stirred by their scandalously handsome captain! Her creamy skin flushed with indignation as the arrogant devil bullied and taunted her. But when he silenced her protests with a conquering kiss, she couldn't help but consider how enjoyable surrender might be!

Hidden Treasure
Raider Prescott had a bad feeling about his beautiful hostage from the start. She was altogether too spirited for her own good...and too desirable for his! When he finally discovered she had no wealthy family to pay for her release, it was more than he could stand. He would take the only riches she could offer -the tantalizing gleam in her golden eyes, the silken splendor of her luscious curves, the priceless treasure of her loving heart. For suddenly he realized that nothing was worth more to him than taking her as Passion's Ransom.

Despite its back cover's claims to the contrary, readers of Betina M. Krahn's *Passion's Ransom* are predisposed to believe that the novel's protagonist, Blythe Woolrich, was simply born to be abducted. Possessed of a "tiny waist," "annoyingly full breasts," and "voluminous brown mane" (14-15), Blythe is a no-nonsense store proprietor whose business acumen is eclipsed by her unfortunate bad luck for meeting all sorts of rogues. Foiling a previous would-be abductor's advances, Blythe is soon thereafter kidnapped by the aptly named Raider Prescott, whose incessant protests that he is not a pirate, but rather a "colonial privateer" are routinely belied by his actions.

Curiously, the novel is obsessed with Raider's piratical status, with frequent deliberations on the matter peppered throughout ("The 'gentleman' and the 'pirate' in him were enraged in a pitched battle for control of his responses" [179]; "Yes, he certainly was a pirate...one who pillaged and devoured her, but was too much of a gentleman to actually do it on the dining room table. Heaven help her, she wanted them both -refined, gentlemanly...'Well, you get to be a pirate sometimes.' She sent a mischievous hand down his lean hip to encourage his hardening manhood..." [420]; "'Hoistin' a stripped jack don't exactly make us 'sons o' liberty,' Bastian objected. 'We sail for ourselfs and ain't never paid no percentage...that makes us *pirates* old son!'....'We prey on British ships only, because I like these brawling colonies -we're *privateers*'" [56 emphases in original]). Blythe reaches a similar conclusion, albeit by different criteria ("'Pirates?' she snorted. 'In a pig's eye. You're not pirates, pirates aren't...' she swallowed back the word 'handsome.' 'They don't -' she almost said, 'speak gentlemanly English'" [85]).

Raider's early assertions that he does not plan to rape Blythe ("'Hush silly woman, I'm not here to ravish you'" [74]; "'Believe me, Wool-witch, nothing could be further from my mind than taking liberties with your...precious person'" [77]) are suspicious in the extreme. Representative is the following exchange which perfectly encapsulates the character's vacillating longings and the novel's own strained logic: "'But my family.' Blythe came to the edge of her chair. 'They need me.' '*I* need you Wool-witch...in my bed!...And I won't be denied.' 'But it's not right, keeping me here against my will...[yet] I do want you [too], Raider...I want to watch you and touch you and want to learn all about you. And I can't help wanting the pleasure you make for me in your bed. You make me feel...beautiful. I've never felt beautiful before'" (239-40 emphasis in original).

Passion's Ransom is unique in its explicit engagement with socio-economic politics. Whereas most novels fail to venture into the intricacies of mercantile capitalism, *Passion's Ransom*'s narrative is grounded in the economic realities eighteenth century trans-Atlantic overseas trade. The ransom to which the title refers drives the story's plot; Blythe's recently impoverished family is unable to pay off her kidnappers, which justifies her prolonged capture. The effect is considerable. Once Raider's motives are mercantile as well as sexual, the economic emphasis aids in Raider's characterization as not being a simple lustful pirate.

In this regard *Passion's Ransom* conforms closely to its ancient Greek counterpart. In these novels, pirates are motivated by both sexual and economic desires. In Xenophon of Ephesus' *Ephesian Tale*, for example, Anthia's captors are seeking hordes of gold and silver and hand her over to merchants in Alexandria for a large sum: "They looked after her at great expense and lavished attention on her appearance, always looking for a buyer at a suitable price. And sure enough someone did come to Alexandria....[who] saw Anthia at the merchant's quarters, was ravished at the sight of her, paid the merchants a large sum, and took her as a maidservant. The moment he bought her the barbarian tried to force her and have his will with her" (153).

Another shared plot device between Passion's Ransom and the Greek novella is the role of gossip regarding the violated heroine being "spoiled goods." Being the exemplary respectable woman, Blythe's concern for her honorable reputation is paramount. Although townsfolk are never given occasion to gossip about her (the overwhelming bulk of the narrative takes place on ship), the querulous land-dwellers in the *Ephesian Tale* have ample opportunity: "'Shameless woman,' she [Rhenaea] said, 'plotting against my marriage! You attracted Polyidus in vain, for you will gain nothing from your good looks; perhaps you were able to entice the pirates and sleep with a horde of young drunkards, but you will not get away with insulting Rhenaea's bed!'" (161-62).

Magic Embrace
Enchanted by a liar
When the infamous pirate Black Garrett learned his brother had been murdered because of a flirtatious chit, the surly rogue swore revenge. Tracking down the worthless wench, Garrett stole her stole her aboard his vessel, planning to ruin her reputation and use her brutally. But as the enraged male rudely kissed her lips and roughly felt her curves, he was transformed by her innocent response. Cursing himself for caring, Black Garrett relentlessly pleasured his captive...and swore she'd feel the lash of his fury the following night!

Hypnotized by a Cad
Bewildered and betrayed, sable-haired Juliet Stoddard had no idea why the terrifying buccaneer had kidnapped her, promising punishment worse than death. Although she had no experience with men, he seemed convinced she was a brazen hussy, and ignored her pleas for mercy. Then the blue-eyed beauty felt Black Garrett's hands where no one had ever touched her before, and she nearly swooned with fear...and desire. Hating the scoundrel, and herself even more, Juliet was powerless to escape this devil's sensual torture and wrest free of his Magic Embrace.

If *Passion's Ransom* goes to considerable pains to characterize Raider Prescott as not "just a pirate," *Magic Embrace* shows no such anxiety. Both novels, however, evidence the same concern that the "lovemakings" depicted are not acts of rape. And yet they are. Whereas (to the best of my recollection) *Passion's Ransom* makes no overt reference to rape ("ravish" is the preferred euphemism), *Magic Embrace* makes ample use of the word. When Garrett first commands Juliet to undress, she steels herself for the worst ("Rape...this rutting...His hands would come on her person. He would be quick to hurt her. It would be over quickly...quickly...." [75]) before he withdraws, protesting "'God's curse, girl, I cannot hurt you...I want to but I can't. Your beauty has bewitched me as surely as my panther, Tonali, himself" (76).

What follows is reminiscent of *Passion's Ransom's* disturbing logic whereby the heroine desires her rapist, despite her feeble protests. I preserve the narrative in all its bewildering, convoluted glory:

"'Oh no...please!...I can't do this....Stop it, stop-'....He felt a primitive, carnal force, a need to possess and own, to claim her in a way that existed two worlds or more from any thought of revenge. Yet he could not continue while thinking of what this meant, so the thought vanished the moment he took her mouth beneath his again. The kiss was long and hard and rapturous, stifling any last thought of struggling. Stifling any last thought. She forgot she was naked, that his belt buckle pressed painfully against her midsection....'Oh please,' she said, biting her lip hard, confused and afraid, 'What do you mean to do by this?'....'Why, I mean to possess you, love. With or without this pretense of innocence, I mean to possess you.'...'Nooo! No, stop!'....'Don't fight me. You'll only prolong my pleasure'" (77-79).

After reading such complicated protests-turned- acquiescence, the pleas of the ancient heroines are refreshingly straightforward. Representative is Xenophon of Ephesus' *Ephesian Tale*, wherein Anthia protests simply: "Whoever you are, take away all this finery; take all there is and everything that is buried with me, but spare my body" (152). Compared to the modern romances' will-they/won't they? (of course they will!) plot structure, the reader of the ancient novella can expect that ultimately the protagonist will ultimately escape his/her abduction undefiled. The threat of piracy looms large. At one point in the *Ephesian Tale*, for instance, a crowd somewhat gratuitously exclaims "Happy are those who will be lucky enough to die without suffering the pirates' chains and seeing themselves the slaves of pirates!" (137). Narrative convention, however, ensures that the lover's chastity is protected. As Witmarsh observes in regards to *Daphnis and Chloe*, "since romance pirates are always carrying romance heroes off to far-away places, the kidnapping of Daphnis seems for a moment to promise sea voyages and high adventure; but the gravitational pull of the pastoral world reasserts itself, and Daphnis is soon back in rural Lesbos." (2008: 110). Expected turns of plot, then, assure readers that the novel's protagonists will find marital fulfillment by the novel's closure, whether they marry their captor or beloved.

I conclude by noting the most glaring difference between ancient and modern romances in terms of narrative conventions - the pirate's omnisexual objects of desire. Although modern mass market romances are of course heterosexist in the extreme, pirates in the Greek novellas are equally interested in male and female captors. In other words, whereas pirates in the ancient Greek novels find homosexual rape to be fair game, their modern counterparts show no similar proclivity. In Longus' *Daphnis and Chloe*, for instance: "When the pirates saw a young man who was tall and handsome and worth more than the plunder from the fields, they didn't waste any more energy on the goats or on the rest of the fields but drown him down to the ship" (301)." Although pirates in modern romance novels do on occasion abduct men, their sexual exploitation is never specified (the closest analogue that I have found is Jean Innes' *Buccaneer's Bride*, which mentions the abduction of "young boys" [84] and "[fine and] dandy folk" [15]; the terms are perhaps meant to be teasingly effete. On the contrary, Sonya T. Pelton's *Windswept Passion* seems to imply that pirates prey on females exclusively: "'Do these pirates take captives -female?' 'Of course. What other captives would be so delightful?...Usually they -pirate captains - will return all the Spanish females they capture. It's sad because the women are usually used goods by then'" (163). This stark contrast between equally opportunistic pirates and modern swashbucklers provides readers interesting food for thought about gender assumptions in contemporary mass market fiction.

Six

Hysterical Women and their Toys

We shall presently draw upon the field of the social history of medicine in order to provide a framework for understanding how the constructions of health and illness served to police the bodies of women in the classical world. Before we begin, let us first ask ourselves the question: how are we to read ancient accounts of women, illness, and healing? I would respond with at least four answers: Firstly, we must never loose sight of the fact that our own takes on medicine are indeed our own. Secondly, we must also be mindful of the fact that our extant ancient texts are themselves also socially conditioned. That is to say that our ancient documents do not provide the anxious researcher with unobjective data to be read independently from their historical circumstances. Thirdly, one has to distinguish between different literary genera and types of evidence. Medical texts written by a circle of physicians will differ from historiography which will in turn differ from religious texts and magical healing spells. And fourthly, one must read ancient medicine within a wider holistic frame of worldviews, including mythology, gender and sex, human and animal nature, cosmography, and the elements. An overview of the ancient medical profession is also needed to provide a cultural context, to which we now turn.

MEDICINE AND ILLNESS IN THE GRECO-ROMAN WORLD

Our earliest sources indicate that the physician was afforded a relatively high status in Antiquity. Among a catalogue of those assembled for the attack on Troy, Homer describes two noble sons of a physician who apparently carried on their father's vocation (Il. 2.728-33). Homer describes the physician as an honored craftsman (*demiourgos*) who practiced his healing for public benefit (*Od.* 17.383). Whereas the physician in Homer appears to be itinerant and likely to practice their craft in public, in later centuries he was to become a functionary within a feudal household. In this regard it appears that the wealthy elite had a greater degree of access to medical care than did the populace at large. There exist some statements encouraging physicians against charging a patient more than they could bear (*Precepts* 4-6; *Decorum* 2); it is unknown, however, how far doctors heeded this advice (McKweon 2002: 54).

Some doctors received their payment from the state. Having a learned doctor in residence could enhance a town's prestige in much the same way as having a famous poet, and the wealthiest city-states competitively vied for the most celebrated healers. Doctors in residence were also invaluable should the city-state be marshaled to war. It is doubtful that doctors in residence indiscriminately healed all of their city-state's populace regardless of social class. Healthcare was primarily a resource for the wealthy clientele possessed with the means to consult physicians and implement prescribed regiments. Some forms of treatment, especially trips to spas and mineral springs, would have been beyond reach of the poor. Celus, for example, prescribes that in order to cure various forms of pestilence his wealthy aristocratic clients ought to take a sea voyage or arrange to be carried about in a litter in order to avoid fatigue (2.17-21). Similarly, highly regimented prescribed diets often comprised of luxury items would require significant discretionary income. While most of the clientele would seem to have been wealthy, some slaves are also mentioned in medical texts; presumably either the slave was wealthy enough to finance their own healthcare or their master was protecting a valuable investment.

There was no division between secular medicine and divine ministrations. Since illness, like most misfortunes, was often perceived as punishment from the gods, it follows that the medical and divine spheres should be intertwined. A number of deities, especially Apollo and Asclepius, had healing powers, and a number of temples of Asclepius, notably at Cos and Pergamum, became major centers of medicine. Gifts were offered to the gods so that the offended deity would forgive the patient. Common religious diagnoses of illness included oracular visions and a more specialized form of divination whereby models of diseased organs were consulted for pertinent information. Doctors not only enlisted the aid of priests and priestesses when diagnosing a patient, but they themselves served religious functions in the temple including dream interpretation and divination. The very language of medicine was imbued with divine imagery; "God-language" was often used to express medical thought, and the lines between prayer, magic, and institutionalized medical care are entirely blurred.

Institutionalized Greco-Roman healthcare was profoundly indebted to pre-Ptolemaic and post-Ptolemaic Egyptian medicine. Early Egyptian medicine is known to us through the Edwin Smith, Ebers, and Chester Beatty papyri (17th, 16th, and 12th centuries BCE respectively), a number of texts which systematically prescribe various surgeries, recipes, and incantations. Scholars unanimously agree that both these early medical traditions and later Hellenistic practices directly influenced Greco-Roman medicine via the prestigious medical schools established in Alexandria (King 2001:6 22). Alexander's conquests sparked considerable interest in and remarkable accession of new information on the curative properties of various plants, minerals, and animals, and established trade routes facilitated the importation of these foreign medicinal substances into Alexandria.

The medical men of Alexandria, however, were celebrated more for their contributions in anatomy and physiology than in pharmacology. They established in the third century BCE an outstanding medical school that combined traditional Egyptian practices with contemporary investigations, heatedly debating the various merits and significance of earlier "irrational" pharaonic medicine against the new "rational" approaches. Alexandrian doctors pioneered the sciences of human anatomy and animal vivisection; the extent to which these anatomists owed to Egyptian mummifiers is an area of scholarly contention (Nutton 1995: 33). Royal support for these (perceived) advances in medicine was provided in providing the bodies of condemned criminals for experiment and state funding that financed medical research as a testament to Hellenized Egypt's cultural supremacy.

While Greco-Roman medicine was heavily influenced by Egyptian practice, the Hippocratic doctors - Greece's most celebrated and prolific medical school - sharply distinguished themselves over and against rival Alexandrian schools via complex and convoluted arguments that differentiated between various approaches to diagnosis. The so-called "dogmatists" were those who relied on the knowledge of hidden causes of disease. The diagnoses and cures resulting from this theoretical frame relied heavily on divination and supplication before the gods. The dogmatists were also greatly influenced by contemporary philosophy, contending that observable phenomena must be supplemented by reasoning and conjecture. In contrast, the "empiricists", while conceding that the gods were indeed active in promoting illness, firmly held that it was neither "legitimate nor necessary to speculate about such matters....[insisting that] the invisible cannot be known: the doctor's task is to treat individual cases, and for this purpose he must avoid inference and attend to, and be directly guided by, the manifest symptoms of the patient and these alone" (Kee 1986: 32).

Despite mutual polemical charges of charlatanism, both the Alexandrian and Hippocratic schools, while differing in approach, shared the same basic perceptions of healing and illness. The healthy body was one which was in perfect equilibrium with the wider natural world, and the doctor's task was to restore their patient's balance within the cosmos and organic health. The conception of health was that of "the harmonic soul and harmonic organism or simply the right combination. Hence should both be trained and balanced.... Disease is then when such disturbances of the harmony become chronic, i.e. when the organism is in an unnatural state" (Ostenfeld 1998: 156). Illness (*nosos*) was equated with *stasis* (discord) and directly connected with the health of the city-state at large. Illness of the individual was alternatively cause or symptom of much wider civil strife, political unrest, and popular agitation.

Informed analysis of disease involved a complete survey of the patient's individual constitution and wider natural world, including information about race, location, climate, and water supply. Health was a state of harmony dependent upon complete harmony of a number of abstract distinctions such as hot/cold, wet/dry, four elements (fire, air, water, earth), and humours (blood, phlegm, yellow bile, and black bile). Health became a sort of democracy and "disease was a 'monarchy' in which an excess of one quality overwhelmed the other" (King 1998: 8). The physician's task was to determine how to best bring these various excesses into a harmonious whole. The most common forms of treatment were diet and exercise intended to restore the balance of bodily humours.

Leaking Bodies

It is only after this lengthy detour that we can approach our specific topic at hand. The doctors of the Hippocratic corpus mention fewer female than male patients; less than one-fourth of Book II, for instance, details the treatment of women. The bulk of women's treatment was overwhelmingly related to sex - in both senses of biological sex, and physical intercourse, and our extant medical discourse on women is almost entirely a discourse on female genitalia and female deficiencies in nature. The ability to procreate was of chief concern to our male writers, and menstruation, vaginal bleeding, and the best times and ages for ensuring fertility were much discussed. Soranus, for instance, disapproves of prepubertal marriage, arguing that it results in precarious pregnancies: "It is good to preserve the state of virginity until menstruation begins by itself. For this will be a definite sign that the uterus is already able to fulfill its proper

function" (*Gyn.* 1.33). In contrast, a Hippocratic doctor enthusiastically prescribes prepubertal intercourse for the release of unwonted pressure on the girl's organs (*Diseases of Young Girls* 8.466-70).

The Hippocratics thought that a woman's overall health was chiefly effected by her womb and menses; proper flow of menstrual blood and internal balance of the womb made it possible for a woman to maintain her health. Unfortunately there existed a number of seemingly interchangeable terms for a woman's womb, vagina, and uterus - all of which carried a nebulous semantic range and uncertain meaning. The Hippocratics referred to the womb as a "vessel" (*aggos*) or "wineskin" (*askos*) waiting to be filled, imagining the womb as having the capacity to expand to contain the fetus in pregnancy. The womb was described as having two "horns" (*kerata*) - not a reference to the Fallopian tubes (unknown to the Hippocratics), but to what seem to have been thought of as two pockets within the womb of tapering structure. The most common female disease - *usterikos* - an illness originating in the womb was occasionally semantically equivalent with the womb (*ustere*) itself. The model of the woman's body was of a network of channels leading to the womb from all over the body; a wide number of fluids including menstrual blood, tears, and liquid biles could all flow across these channels and either drain out of the womb or remain and fester. Because the womb provided doctors with an additional orifice to study, the woman's body - to the trained eye - could be better comprehended. While the human body was difficult to read, "by providing an extra sign to examine, women's bodies are easier to understand" (King 1998: 53).

It is crucial that we understand woman's bodies and illnesses in light of Greco-Roman cosmography as a whole. Women were regarded as inherently unstable and lacking in the ability to control their own boundaries. The female body was amorphous and wet in nature, as opposed to the superior dry male body (*Epidemics* 4.1, Aristotle *Probl.* 4.25.879a33-34, Galen 1.765. Homer describes Zeus as dry in *Il.* 14.165). Hippocrates contended that "the female flourishes more in an environment of water, from things cold and wet and soft, whether food or drink or activities. The male flourishes more in an environment of fire, from dry, hot foods and mode of life" (*Vict.* 27). Owing, in part, to their wet nature, women were also soft (*malakos*) and thus lacking in manly fortitude (*Diseases of Women 1*, *Diseases of Young Girls* 1, *Regimen* 1.27). A woman's innate wetness characterized her as perpetually unstable and irrational, as her body was in constant battle to maintain some semblance of balance and order.

Wetness and softness resulted in a fundamental inconstancy; a body's softness made it as porous, malleable, and inconstant as a sponge. *Diseases of Women* begins (1.1) with an attempt to root female disease in female wetness and instability, starting from the premise that women are softer, and then arguing that as wool - a porous, soft substance - absorbs more liquid than do denser fabrics - so too do woman's bodies soak up liquid. Women are not only wet, they leak as well. A woman's body is a leaky vessel characterized by a constant draining, perpetual motion, amorphous boundaries, and additional channels and orifices for fluid(ity). As noted by Anne Carson: "women are formless creatures who cannot or will not or do not maintain their own boundaries and who are awfully adept at confounding the boundaries of others" (1990: 155). Health, for women, was largely a matter of making a woman as much of a man as possible. Manly activities, games, exercise, and diet were routinely prescribed as medical therapy for women in order to dry, harden, and reshape their bodies into better harmony with the universe (*Gyn.*, Gal. 5.899-910). As constructed by medical discourse, then, by being healed - literally dried up - the woman was made drier (more male) and less prone to leakage (less female). It is this discourse of the female body that leads me to conclude that the entire Hippocratic corpus can be seen as an attempt at the hegemonic control of women.

GOOD VIBRATIONS

The Hippocratic discourse on the wondering womb has enjoyed a regrettably long shelf-life; variants of the theory and its cures persisted well into modernity, and are perhaps still discernible in contemporary rhetoric on female irrationality, Post Menopausal Syndrome, etc. By means of a conclusion I would like to consider more recent effects of the wondering womb, and the surprising medical treatments proscribed by the medical profession. In so doing I hope to offer a window into the spell which classical Antiquity has cast over the millennia.

In her erudite study of the technological effects of the wondering womb, Rachel Maines has reconstructed the ways in which hysteria served as a paradigm for female illness (1995: 7). Owing to the "vague and sexually focused character of hysteria as defined by ancient, medieval, Renaissance, and modern medical authorities before Sigmund Freud," Maines demonstrates how doctors were able to diagnose the wondering womb as the cause of a wide number of female illnesses such as anxiety, sleeplessness, and nervousness (1995: 7-11). The considerable impact of general Greco-Roman medicine on the Western world is an old story; more amazing are the specific consequences of the wondering womb.

Beginning at least in the seventeenth century, the medical profession most often prescribed masturbation (at times professionally-assisted) as an effective cure for female hysteria. To take but one example, in 1653 Pieter van Foreest published a medical compendium recommending that one ask a medical professional to "massage the genitalia with one finger inside, using oil of lilies, musk root, crocus, or [something] similar….in this way the afflicted woman can be aroused to paroxysm. This kind of stimulation is recommended by Galen and Avicenna…." (Maines 1995: 1). Whether from prudery or cramped fingers, doctors earnestly sought out and invented mechanisms to induce female orgasm in the cure for hysteria; they found a ready market for their products. With the advent of electricity (and later the battery), hydriatic, foot-pedaled, and steam-powered massagers gave way to the portable female vibrator (Maines 1995: 12-20).

Suffice it to say that the vibrator has since made its way out of the hospital and into the bedrooms of satisfied women. I close with this tangential historical footnote not (in the eyes of one reviewer) to provide scintillating detail or to sell more copies, but rather to chart a trajectory which illustrates the possibility for hegemonic discourse to make way for liberatory practices. In this one instance, at least, an unfortunate staple of the classical tradition has found a more suitable end. Yet one need not go so far afield; one of our earliest Greek writers found ways to rethink phallocentric paradigms of womanhood. To return briefly once more to Sappho, let us consider my favorite fragment, 166: "They do say that once upon a time Leda found an egg hidden in the hyacinth" (*Phaisi de pota Ledan uakinthoi pepukadmenon / Euren oion*).

In an extraordinary feat of revisionist mythology, Sappho has completely retold the story of Leda, mother of Helen of Troy. In the canonical version Leda was raped by Zeus who took the form of a swan. In fragment 166, however, Leda is not the victim of rape, but rather a woman who actively searches out (*maiomai* "I search out by feeling, I ferret,") and nurtures an egg which represents both Helen and her own clitoris hidden under the labia

(Winkler 1990: 184). With a stunning economy of words, Sappho has replaced patriarchal discourse with a celebration of autonomous female sexuality, offering new ways for her readers to consider ancient Greek thought.

SEVEN

EHUD THROUGH THE LOOKING GLASS

WITH THE NOTABLE EXCEPTION OF Deconstruction, modern Semiotic theory is perhaps the most esoteric of all academic disciplines. What follows is a semiotic reading of Judges 3; in an effort to make semiotics (the study of words and signs) a bit more approachable, I preface this study with a reading of two beloved children's books - Lewis Carroll's *Alice Through the Looking Glass* and Roald Dahl's *BFG* - that offer useful entrees to the vagaries of this rarified field.

Alice Through the Looking Glass

While in the Looking-Glass House, Alice has a curious encounter with the White King, during which his Majesty struggles to put thought to paper, finally blaming his choice of medium: "'My dear! I really *must* get a thinner pencil. I can't manage this one a bit; it writes all manner of things that I don't intend'" (101). While fretting over the King's failed attempt at writing, Alice soon experiences literary confusion of her own. Alice spies a book lying on a nearby table, "and while she sat watching the White King (for she was still a little anxious about him, and had the ink all ready to throw over him, in case he fainted again), she turned over the leaves, to find some part that she could read, 'for it's all in some language I don't know,' she said to herself" (101). The text she encounters reads:

YKCOWREBBAJ

sevot yhtils eht dna ,gillirb sawT`
ebaw eht ni elbmig dna eryg diD
,sevogorob eht erew ysmim llA
.ebargtuo shtar emom eht dnA

Alice puzzles over the poem for some time before finally "a bright thought struck her. 'Why, it's a Looking-glass book, of course! And if I hold it up to a glass, the words will all go the right way again" (101). Unfortunately, Alice's discovery does little to rectify her conclusion. When she reads the text in its entirety, she is presented with Carroll's celebrated Jabberwocky poem:

JABBERWOCKY

`Twas brillig, and the slithy toves
Did gyre and gimble in the wabe;
All mimsy were the borogoves,
And the mome raths outgrabe.

`Beware the Jabberwock, my son!
The jaws that bite, the claws that catch!
Beware the Jujub bird, and shun

The frumious Bandersnatch!'

He took his vorpal sword in hand:
Long time the manxome foe he sought --
So rested he by the Tumtum gree,
And stood awhile in thought.

And as in uffish thought he stood,
The Jabberwock, with eyes of flame,
Came whiffling through the tulgey wook,
And burbled as it came!

One, two! One, two! And through and through
The vorpal blade went snicker-snack!
He left it dead, and with its head
He went galumphing back.

'And has thou slain the Jabberwock?
Come to my arms, my beamish boy!
O frabjous day! Calloh! Callay!
He chortled in his joy.

'Twas brillig, and the slithy toves
Did gyre and gimble in the wabe;
All mimsy were the borogoves,
And the mome raths outgrabe (101-02)

The Jabberwocky is Carroll's "double-talk" poem, which, succinctly put is "written in talk that combines nonsense sounds with real words. It sounds like real language" (101). The poem is (to the best of my knowledge) the most challenging piece of text in all of children's literature. Through its nonsense sounds, the reader finds herself in a labyrinth of clues that require active participation in order to decipher its meaning. This is an extreme example of the ways in which *all* texts -in varying degrees to be sure- preclude the lazy reader from appreciating their stabs at human communication. As we shall see presently, texts never offer a clear window with which to view the world. Texts participate in an active discourse of allusions structured upon the reader's expectations. After half a dozen readings, I can only conclude with Alice, who says that the poem "'seems very pretty...but it's *rather* hard to understand!' (You see she didn't like to confess, ever to herself, that she couldn't make it out at all.) 'Somehow it seems to fill my head with ideas -- only I don't exactly know what they are! However, *somebody* killed *something*: that's clear, at any rate – '" (102).

The BFG

In his most famous book, Roald Dahl creates for his *BFG* (Big Friendly Giant) a memorable nonsense language that has delighted children since its publication. Through his use of alliteration and reference-in-context, Dahl offers readers an engaging intellectual puzzle that is less poetical but more easily deciphered than Carroll's Jabberwocky. In the book's most extended display of virtuosity, the BFG explains his cannibalistic diet to the orphan Sophie, who he has recently "kidsnatched" because she accidently saw him. I choose this passage because it provides a useful illustration of one of semiotic's crucial tenets, namely the assertion that if texts are to be understandable, they require active participation on the reader's part. To aid in readability, I offer a series of easily referenced ellipses:

> "'Bonecruncher says Turkish human beans has a glamourly flavour. He says Turks from Turkey is tasting of turkey.'
>
> 'I suppose they would,' Sophie said.
>
> 'Of course they would!' the Giant shouted. 'Every human bean is diddly and different. Some is scrumdiddlyumptious and some is uckyslush. Greeks is all full of uckyslush. No Giants is eating Greeks, ever.'

'Why not?' Sophie asked.

'Greeks from Greece is all tasting greasy,' the Giant said....

'As I am saying,' the Giant went on, 'all human beans is having different flavours. Human beans from Panama is tasting very strong of hats.'"

Like Dahl's own readers, Sophie understands the Giant's jumbled language well enough, but struggles with its content. She promptly asks for clarification:

"'Why hats?' Sophie said.

'You is not very clever,' the Giant said, moving his great ears in and out. 'I thought all human beans is full of brains, but your head is emptier than a bundongle....'

'The human bean,' the Giant went on, 'is coming in dillions of different flavours. For instance, human beans from Wales is tasting very whooshey of fish. There is something very fishy about Wales.'

'You mean whales,' Sophie said. 'Wales is something quite different.'

'Wales is whales,' the Giant said. Don't gobblefunk around with words....I will now give you another example. Human beans from Jersey has a most disgustable wooly tickle on the tongue,' the Giant said. 'Human beans from Jersey is tasting of cardigans.'

'You mean jerseys,' Sophie said.

'You are once again gobblefunking!' the Giant shouted. 'Don't do it! This is a serious and snitching subject. May I continue?'

'Aren't you getting a bit mixed up?' Sophie said.

'I is a very mixed up Giant,' the Giant said. "But I does do my best.'"

SEMIOTICS AND JUDGES 3

In his insightful article "Cruising as Methodology", Timothy Koch argues for an inclusive approach to scripture which might make space for queer readings of the Bible: "...an approach that we *each* base on our own erotic knowledge allows us *all* to pursue that which catches our eye, which calls to us, which holds out at least the hope of connection and transformation..." (2001:180, emphases in original). Following his call to cruise the scriptures for queer readings, Koch lists Judg. 3:12-26 among several biblical passages that seem (for him) to be pregnant with homoerotic connotation. Before reviewing Koch's arguments for homoerotic undertones in this passage, let us first acquaint ourselves with the text:

The Israelites again did what was evil in the sight of the LORD; and the LORD strengthened King Eglon of Moab against Israel, because they had done what was evil in the sight of the LORD. In alliance with the Ammonites and the Amalekites, he went and defeated Israel; and they took possession of the city of palms. So the Israelites served King Eglon of Moab eighteen years.

But when the Israelites cried out to the LORD, the LORD raised up for them a deliverer, Ehud son of Gera, the Benjaminite, a left-handed man. The Israelites sent tribute by him to King Eglon of Moab. Ehud made for himself a sword with two edges, a cubit in length; and he fastened it on his right thigh under his clothes. Then he presented the tribute to King Eglon of Moab. Now Eglon was a very fat man.

When Ehud had finished presenting the tribute, he sent the people who carried the tribute on their way. But he himself turned back at the sculptured stones near Gilgal, and said, "I have a secret message for you, O king." So the king said, "Silence!" and all his attendants went out from his presence.

Ehud came to him, while he was sitting alone in his cool roof chamber, and said, "I have a message from God for you." So he rose from his seat.

Then Ehud reached with his left hand, took the sword from his right thigh, and thrust it into Eglon's belly; the hilt also went in after the blade, and the fat closed over the blade, for he did not draw the sword out of his belly; and the dirt came out.

Then Ehud went out into the vestibule, and closed the doors of the roof chamber on him, and locked them. After he had gone, the servants came. When they saw that the doors of the roof chamber were locked, they thought, "He must be relieving himself in the cool chamber." So they waited until they were embarrassed. When he still did not open the doors of the roof chamber, they took the key and opened them. There was their lord lying dead on the floor. Ehud escaped while they delayed, and passed beyond the sculptured stones, and escaped to Seirah. Judg. 3:12-26 NRSV

Koch puts forth a number of observations in support his homoerotic reading of the passage. Koch's suggestions might be summarized as follows:

-Ehud is left-handed. Upon defecating, the left hand was used in Ancient Near Eastern cultures for cleaning the anus.
-"A 'cubit" (roughly eighteen inches) would certainly be an impressive measurement for *anything* found snaking down (okay, okay, 'fastened' to) a young man's right thigh!"
-Ehud purposefully manipulated his audience with the king to effect a private seduction.
-It was the promise of Ehud's eighteen-inch member that prompted King Eglon to grant Ehud a private audience.
In Koch's analysis, then, it is both Ehud's possession of a prodigious member and his being left-handed that form the foci of homoeroticism.

Since my own reading of Judg. 3:12-26 differs markedly from Koch's, rather than provide an in-depth analysis of Koch's claims the present study will answer his invitation to "cruise the scripture" for queer readings of the Bible. Using Koch's suggestions as points of departure, I will here examine Judg. 3:12-26, drawing upon postmodern insights of semiotics to analyze the erotic undertones of the passage. It is my explicit thesis that Judg. 3:12-26 contains a number of semiotic hints and allusions which guide the reader toward a homoerotic interpretation of the passage. I also aim to investigate the extent to which this passage served as invective against male-male anal sex by situating the text against similar First Testament narratives of male-male rape (Gen. 19, Judg. 19).

SIGNS, TEXTS, AND MEANING

Semiotics is the analysis of signs and meanings. In this definition the "sign" refers to a linguistic or sensory unit which signifies something to somebody while the "meaning" references a *possible* interpretation by a *possible* interpreter. I take as my starting point the contention that every text is encoded with signs; signs which must be interpreted by the reader if the text is to be made understandable. Neither texts nor the words they employ factually communicate by offering a clear window with which to view the world. On the contrary, both texts and words engage in a manipulated discourse of misinformation structured upon guiding the reader/hearer's expectations and interpretation. Every text is polysemic and open to a number of (re) interpretations; each time the text is read/heard it is reimagined with unique distinctions made by the reader/hearer and her community.

And yet no text is entirely open-ended but rather crafted to guide the reader toward a particular interpretation. Every text is both a synthesis of signs and an instrument of persuasion. Texts are comprised of signs. The signs that underwrite a text are as numerous as their motives, and as thoroughly naturalized within the culture that generates and exploits them. Signs are never free of their cultural context, nor are they free of the motives of their users, but are instead wholly dependent on conventions and the extent to which they meaningfully relate to other signs in turn. No sign explains itself, and no text composed of signs can be understood by those who remain unable to decipher its codes; Wood and Fels explain that even the most "obvious" or "transparent" of signs are unable to effectually communicates themselves; its not so much that texts need to be *de*coded "but that they are by and large *en*coded in signs....Signs are not signs for, dissolve into marks for, those who don't know the code" (Wood and Fels 1986: 54-58).

In light of an understanding of the function of signs it becomes clear that texts do not innocently tell stories as it might have previously been supposed. Because texts constitute a semiological system they are in constant danger of seizure by interpretations foreign to the author(s)' agendas. To safeguard against wayward interpretation and ensure a "correct" reading, texts insidiously hide their motives while pretending to be neutral. In his groundbreaking analysis of sign-as-myth, Roland Barthes contends that texts "naturalize" their signs and meanings: "what allows the reader to consume myth innocently is that he does not see it as a semiological system but as an inductive one" (Barthes 1972: 131). It is the text's position of neutrality and objectivity that allows it to tendentiously convey meaning as it unfolds through a cycle of interpretation each time it is picked up by a reader.

Every text is thus an illusion, a cultural artifact encoded through an accumulation of choices made among choices (to utilize x instead of y in such a manner so as to convey meanings and guide particular interpretations). There is no self-explanatory text, just as there exists no self-explanatory sign. However obvious they might appear, all signs are determined by social rule. Texts are comprised of rhetorical codes that serve to orient the document in its culture; the meaning and use of texts is set in a cultural context of values and beliefs that reinforce and re-inscribe the values and culturally-determined meanings of their culture.

The reader plays a demonstrably active role in the processes of interpretation. Every text relies on a reader to actualize its meaning; "Every text is a lazy machine asking the reader to do some of its work" (Eco 1984: 80). Each text is inscribed with the role of the Ideal Reader, the Reader who will perfectly aid in the text's actualization by fully capitulating with the author's textual strategy and thus interpreting the work in complete harmony with the text's agendas. Wolfgang Iser has helpfully built upon Eco's insights to situate the role of actual readers with their encountered texts. Iser holds that textually speaking the (actual) reader's role is significantly impacted by the construction of the Ideal Reader which serves to manipulate the (actual) reader towards alignment with the text's semiological agenda (1978: 35).

Every text has a pre-text and a post-text. As the (actual) reader encounters a sign (and every letter, word, image is a sign), she must interpret that sign in light of its cultural convention. A history of a word's usage, its meaning, symbolism, and import are continuously being juggled in the reader's mind as the sign's meaning is being determined. This is an ongoing process; each sign is analyzed in its own right and then made meaningful with the text as a whole as it is related to the constituent signs of its narrative. The reader must relate every sign to its use in previous texts and discourse. As the reader determines the meaning of a given sign in relation to its meta-text and pre-texts, the reader effects a very real power over the interpretive process.

This is not, however, an unbounded process. Eco reminds us that "the interpreted text imposes some constraints upon its interpreters" (1990: 7). Firstly, the reader is constantly being guided to a "correct" interpretation through the text's pleas for internal coherence. Signs must be situated with related textual signs in such a way that makes sense of the work as a whole. Secondly, the reader is forced to interpret each sign in keeping with their cultural context if the sign is to remain commonsensical. Therefore social convention also dictates a proper reading of a text and shapes its reading. Although the reader is invited into an active role in the interpretive process they are constrained by textual and cultural limitations that preclude them from violating semiotic convention.

HOMOEROTICISM AND JUDG. 3:12-26

And what has all of this to do with the text at hand? It is my contention that through a carefully constructed use of signs the author(s) of Judg. 3:12-26 shaped his narrative in such a way that would guide the text's readers toward a homoerotic understanding of Ehud's murder of Eglon. Timothy Koch has already identified Eglon's possible delight in Ehud's eighteen inch penis, a phallus which unfortunately (for the king) turns out in fact to be a two-edged sword. In addition to Koch's suggestion I will now set forth a number of signs which I deem to be lexically significant, arguing that through intertextual echoes and semantic range the author of Judges 3 leads his reader to a sexual interpretation of these verses.

I find the locus of Eglon's penetration, the *biten* - "belly" to be highly suggestive of male-male anal sex. The term *btn* ("body" "belly" "womb " BDB 105) covers a wide semantic range but seems to be entirely restricted to the corporeal realm and is frequently used to contrast physicality with the intangible soul (Ps. 31:10). The precise identification of which of Eglon's innards are being penetrated remain purposefully ambiguous, almost teasingly so in a manner which begs for further deliberation and musing. The author(s) of Judg. 3 choose to describe Eglon's inner cavities with a word often meant to connote sexual reproduction (i.e. Gen. 25:23, 38:27; Job 3:10, 10:19; Ps. 132:11; Deut. 7:13, 28:4, 30:9).

Through intratextual context the site of Eglon's penetration is further illuminated by the narrator's description that "the dirt came out" of the wound (3:22). As already noted, Ehud's description as a "left-handed man" (3:15) has already prepared the reader for an association of the left hand with the removal of feces and therefore by extension the anus and anal sex. Furthermore, the word translated by the NRSV as "dirt" is a *hapax legomena* in our Hebrew corpus. The term is most often taken to relate to *peres* "faecal matter" (BDB 831). Michael Barré has argued that the term also relates to the Akkadian verb *naparsudu* which can refer to the escaping of feces from bowels (Barré 1991:229-45). Gregory Mobley supports Barré's claim by noting that such a reading "prepares us, as the story does in so many other particulars, for a later development; in this case, the guards' assumption that their king was defecating. *Parsed,* whether from Hebrew *peres* or Akkadian *prsd* can be etymologically related to words meaning something like 'feces'" (2005:83). The developments which the reading prepares us for are the descriptions of

Ehud and the king's guards "entering" and "exiting" various areas of the palace (3:24, 26).

By describing the wound as near-overflowing with fecal matter, the location of Eglon's penetration is brought more closely into light. The reader is being supplied with clues that rather than factually relating a deathblow transforms the narrative into an act of phallic penetration with the potential for homoerotic undertone. The author's use of *parsed* also clues the attentive reader to the sacrificial imagery of the passage. The term's cognate *peres* is used exclusively in the Hebrew Bible to describe the feces found in the bowels of sacrificial victims. By utilizing intertextual pre-signs the reader's interpretation is shaped to anticipate Ehud's death. The mighty king will be slaughtered like a bull.

This characterization of Ehud as being ripe for the slaughter is further heightened by his physical appearance, first introduced as "now Eglon was a very fat man" (3:17) and then again highlighted "and the fat closed over the blade" (3:22). The word *bari'* is most often used in the First Testament to describe plump animals ready to be sacrificed. Gregory Mobley explains that through these allusions to sacrificial imagery Eglon "is described as a young fleshy animal ripe for slaughtering, a graphic narrative encapsulation of the motif of the ceremonial slaughter of enemy leaders" (2005: 77). Through the relations of intertextual signs and linguistic clues the reader is led to anticipate the king's demise before the murder itself ever occurs.

Another semiotic connection made between male homoeroticism and Eglon's murder is Ehud's characterization of being a Benjaminite (3:15). Intrartextual allusion in the book of Judges links the Benjaminites with male same-sex acts and murder-rape. Chapter 19 of Judges relates the story of a concubine who leaves her Levite man and sets off for her father's house in Bethlehem (Judg. 19:2). Her husband sets off to reclaim his property and is warmly welcomed by his father-in-law who promptly hands over the woman (Judg. 19:3-9). On their return journey home the man and concubine stop for the night in the Benjaminite town of Gibeah where they are invited into the home of a kindly old man (Judg. 19:15).

In the middle of the night a depraved lot of Benjaminites storm the house and demand sexual use of the old man's guest: "Bring out the man who has come into your house, so that we can be intimate with him" (Judg. 19:22). Lest the reader pass over the fact that this mob is comprised of Benjaminite citizens, their identity is further repeated through the emphatic description of the old man's fatherland: "This man hailed from the hill country of Ephraim and resided at Gibeah, where the townspeople were Benjaminites" (Judg. 19:16). Horrified by the mob's demand, the old man pleads: "Please, my friends, do not commit such a wrong. Since this man has entered my house, do not perpetuate this outrage Look, here is my virgin daughter, and his concubine. Let me bring them out to you. Have your pleasure of them, do what you like with them; but don't do that outrageous thing to the man" (Judg. 19:23-24). The concubine is promptly thrown out of the house whereupon she is raped and murdered until daybreak (Judg. 19:25).

In this passage the Benjaminites are graphically depicted as desiring male same-sex rape. Indeed, the mob is described as being unpersuaded by the old man's offer of female substitution and consistently focused on the Levite male (Judg. 19:25). That male homoeroticism is given a negative connotation in this passage is unquestionable. The threat of male rape is so potent that the Levite's host is willing to substitute his own daughter to preserve his guest's honor. Much like the Benjaminites' threat of Judges 19, the unsuspecting, unwilling penetration of Eglon with Ehud's sword can only be described as rape. The left-handed Benjaminite's homoerotic proclivities are semiologically connected with Ehud's left-handedness. Through semiotic connections of pre-texts and post-texts, Ehud's Benjaminite nature leads the reader to interpret Ehud's murder homoerotically via intratextual readings, re-readings, and re-interpretations which situate Judges 3 in light of related semiological domains.

In addition to the aforementioned allusions in Judg. 3, the phallic nature of Ehud's murder weapon and the male agent wielding it contribute to a homoerotic interpretation of the text. Ehud's object of penetration graphically replaces his promised "message from God" (3:19, 20) as the thing to be delivered. Like the sex act, the deathblow culminates in a wet climactic end; Ehud's vigorous thrust of violent penetration can be read as sexual penetration as easily as it can a fatal strike. The sexually domineering nature of the act of penetration with a weapon needs little explanation. The deathblow is a forceful act which takes on a sexualized tone which is heightened by the erotic undercurrents of the narrative. Throughout Judg. 3:12-26 the author manipulates sex and eroticism throughout his narrative, and the manner of Englon's death is no exception.

Although I agree with Robert Alter's (1981: 39) detection of eroticism in the Eglon-Ehud episode, I am intrigued but ultimately unpersuaded by his translation of *dabar elohim* as "secret thing," which for Alter strengthens the homoerotic connotation. I do not see how the phrase can bear the weight of his translation; although I concede that *dabar* can have a secondary meaning of "thing" (BDB 183), its meaning in these instances is emphatically temporal (in the sense of "after these things), not corporeal (see Gen 15:1, 22:1, 40:1; 1 Kgs. 17:17; Ezr 7:1; Est 2:1, 3:1). In Judg. 3:19, 20 the phrase *dabar elohim* is in perfect keeping with its common meaning of word/will of God (see BDB 182 for approximately thirty instances of such usage).

The phrase "and struck him in the belly" occurs with some frequency in First Testament narrative as a description of the climactic fatal strike. The act is always emphatically private and occurs between two men: "*So they went into the house*, as though fetching wheat, and struck him in the belly (2 Sam. 4:6); "When Abner returned to Hebron, Joab took him aside within the gate to talk to him privately; there he struck him in the belly" (2 Sam. 3:27). The verb *tq'* "thrust, clap, give a blow" (BDB 1075) is a stock-phrase denoting the manner of one's death. What most interests me are the parallels and semiotic connections being made in Judg. 3:12-26 between being "struck in the belly" with a sword and being "struck in the belly" as a descriptor of receptive anal sex. Most revealing for our purposes is the observation that in the book of Judges' cultural context the acts of sex, murder, and battle are all zero sum games in which one person's gain is another person's loss.

In his succinct summary of Israel's construction of sex acts as being inherently shaming for one party, Martti Nissinen concludes that Israel, like its neighbors: "shared with its cultural environment an understanding of sexual life as an interaction between active masculine and passive feminine gender roles. This interaction was the cornerstone of gender identity, but the concept of sexual orientation was unknown. Sexual contact between two men was prohibited because the passive party assumed the role of a woman and his manly honor was thus disgraced" (1998:44).

Eastern references to homoeroticism which structure male homoeroticism as emasculating acts centered upon dominance and aggression. To cite a couple of Nisineen's examples: firstly, in the Egyptian Myth of the battle between the two gods Horus and Seth the plot finds the two deities locked in a power struggle for dominion over the Egyptian pantheon. To further his desire for lordship, Seth sexually abuses Horus by anal intercourse in order to force Horus "into the position of a defeated and raped enemy, thus making him unfit for the status of king" (1998:19). Secondly, like the Egyptian Myth of Seth and Horus, the *Middle Assyrian Laws* similarly reflect the belief that the recipient of male-male anal intercourse was shamed and emasculated: "If a man furtively spreads rumors about his comrade, saying: 'Everyone has sex with him', or in a quarrel in public says to him: "Everyone has sex with you), I can prove the charges,' but he is unable to prove the charges and does not prove the charges, they shall strike him 50 blows with the rods..."(1998:25). The internal logic of this edict from the *Middle Assyrian Laws* relies on the conviction that a man accused of receptive anal intercourse would suffer a loss in social standing. To safeguard against spurious accusations of passive same-sex practices, the Laws decree harsh penalties for those who cannot support false claims of such behavior.

THE EROTICS OF VIOLENCE

INVECTIVE AGAINST MALE-MALE COUPLING

All of which brings me to my main point: the inescapable connections in the Israelite semiotic domain between male-male sex and male-male violence. If both sex and death participate in zero-sum games wherein one person's gain is another's loss, the question becomes not "How could the violent death of Eglon at the hands of Ehud's sword be read homoerotically?" so much as "How could Eglon's death *not* be interpreted homoerotically in light of the inescapable Israelite semiological connections between male-male sex and violence?"

In sum, semiotic convention, allusions, and hints guide the reader toward a homoerotic understanding of Ehud's murder of the plump bull ready for slaughter. The interconnections between violence and male-male sex abound in First Testament narrative. Semiotic convention dictates a connection between male-male deathly penetration and the violence of male-male sex acts, acts with fatal outcomes. The semantic range for the site of Eglon's penetration explicitly links the belly with sex acts. Ehud's descriptor as a Benjaminite establishes the hero in semiological relation with Benjaminite kinsmen who actively seek the sexual abuse-death of a Levite man. Both Ehud's left-handedness associating him with the removal of feces and the description of fecal matter escaping Eglon's wound connect the king's death semiotically with the anus, issuing forth a chain of associative resonances - from feces, to anus, to "the lying of men."

In keeping with this book's thematic considerations, it is now time to consider these semiotic connections in a Greco-Roman perspective. How would Jews in Antiquity read/heard this story? What cultural "baggage" did they bring with them that would inform such readings? The penis-as-weapon is one of the oldest, most enduring Roman tropes or phallic aggression. Consider Novius' farcical *Pappus Praeteritus*, which makes the following joke: "As long as you invite those supporters, father, you will put your butt on a sword-hilt before you put it in the magistrate's chair." Craig Williams explains that "with their reference to *suffragatores* (supporters of a candidate for political office) and the *sella curulis* (the official seat used by certain magistrates), together with the metaphorical use of *capulus* ('sword-hilt') to refer to the penis, these lines are utterly Roman in tone, as is their hearty humor at the expense of a man who is, figuratively at least, being anally penetrated" (1999:29). Even more telling are the phallicly shaped lead sling-bullets from the siege of Perugia (ca. 41 B.C.E.) Inscribed with such gems as: "I seek Octavian's asshole"; "Loose Octavius, sit on this;" "Greetings, Octavius: you suck dick;" "Bald Lucius Antonius and Fulvia, open up your asshole."

The interconnections between sex and feces are even more at home in a Greco-Roman milieu. A few examples will suffice. As is so often the case, the phallic god Priapus states the matter most bluntly. Most instructive is *Priapea* 69.4, where the deity advises a potential thief to consider "how heavy a load of dick you will have to shit out" should they be caught stealing from his garden. A line from Lucilius compares the bodies of males and females: "She bloodies you, but he on the other hand beshits you" (trans. Williams 1999: 30, 24 respectively). Consider also Martial's friend Charisianus who complains that he has been unable to have anal sex for some time because he is suffering from diarrhea (Sat. 11.88), or Ausonius' acquaintance who is so fond of anal intercourse with young men that he most likely be reincarnated as a dung beetle (*Epigr.* 77.8).

So, why, then, did the filth come out of Eglon's wound? If my reading of homoeroticism being semiotically encoded in the text of Judges 3 is convincing, we are still left with the question: *why* the inter and intra textual allusions to homoeroticism? Why is Eglon not just killed on the level of narrative but also raped on the level of interpretation? Why the emphasis on feces? I contend that in its cultural context which viewed male-male intercourse as inherently shaming for one partner, the evocative description of Eglon as raped serves to further humiliate the king and signify his complete and utter defeat.

I also contend that the emphasis on feces serves as invective against male-male anal sex. The First Testament descriptions of male homoeroticism previously discussed in this essay are uniformly negative towards the act. The shameful rape of King Eglon is entirely congruent with these negative accounts. Through semiotic clues the reader is guided toward an connection between male-male sex and fecal matter. Our biblical descriptions of *peres* emphasize that the matter is dirty, defiling, and must be eradicated in order to produce clean specimens worthy of religious sacrifice. By engaging with the text of Judges the reader is led to connections between Eglon's death and male same-sex acts, between male same-sex acts and defiling feces.

The Ideal reader is meant to come to the understanding that dirtying homosexual acts are best if avoided. The Suspicious reader, however, can navigate her way through a text's labyrinth of semiological associations in a manner which allows her to approach the text on her terms. After all, texts are not only constructed through actualized encounters, but deconstructed through unique life experiences, different cultural contexts, and critical analysis. I am imagining a textual world free from harmful and petty invective, a space of inclusivity wherein attentive readers are not destined to readily capitulate with authorial aims. A Hermeneutic of Suspicion allows me to read Judges 3 "against the grain", questioning the author's motives and credibility. A Hermeneutics of Desire allows me to read whatever I wish into a text, providing me the space for my own interpretive vision. And a Hermeneutic of Imagination provides me with my point of departure, a site of liberation which refuses to uncritically disseminate agendas of hate. Happily, all three of these interpretative strategies are fully commensurate with our biblical text. These are a few of my strategies, a few of my visions. But I do not presume to dictate either method or desiderata. How will you read Jud. 3? What will you find in the text?

CONCLUSION

THE PRECEDING CHAPTERS HAVE ATTEMPTED to document the simple but crucial fact that sex and gender in the classical world were neither stable nor monolithic constructions. Rather than offer a synthesis of these chapters, I would like to conclude these efforts with a final reconsideration in regards to the often unexamined assumption that Penelope in Homer's *Odyssey* has remained unwavering in her affections for her husband during his prolonged absence. We will take as our starting point Penelope's dream of the geese in Book 19. Although sufficiently mentioned in the *Iliad*, dreams feature much more prominently in the *Odyssey* and are crucial to its plot. As the action of the *Odyssey* moves towards its conclusion, "Homer makes increasing use of omens, prophecies, and dreams to intensify the sense of impending crisis" (Russo 1982: 4). The use of dreams plays a crucial role in the dramatic climax in Book 19, wherein Penelope relates her dream of the slaughtered geese to Odysseus. It is here that dreams convey both explicit and coded messages of sexual longing, marital affection, and maternal love.

During her husband's twenty year absence, Penelope has been plagued by greedy suitors who rival for her husband's throne and her own affections.

During his long absence from home, she forestalled her many suitor's considerable pressures to remarry, and effectively "cheated the heart in the breast of the Achaeans. To all she gives hope and promises each man, sending forth messages (*aggelias*). But in her mind (*noos*) designs other things" (Od. 2.90-92). In an attempt to buy her husband more time, Penelope devises the trick of weaving and unweaving Laertes' shroud while expressing lukewarm interest in her suitors:

> "And this is another trick (*dolon*) she devised in her mind.
> She set up a great loom in the halls and was weaving
> a web both delicate and symmetrical. And then she said to us:
> 'Young men, my suitors, since shining Odysseus has died,
> wait, even though you are eager for my marriage, until I complete this mantle,
> lest my spinning be wasted in vain,
> a shroud for the hero Laertes, for whenever
> the common doom of painful death brings him down,
> lest someone of the Achaean women in the community blame me,
> if he were to lie without a sheet to wind him, he who acquired much'" (*Od.* 2. 93-103).

An unfaithful maid eventually betrays Penelope's ruse, and she is pressured by her suitors to choose a new husband. Happily, Odysseus returns to Ithaca before Penelope is forced to replace him. In order to ascertain his wife's faithfulness, he disguises himself as a beggar and questions Penelope. The conversation that follows concerning Penelope's marital fidelity makes extensive use of dreams and their interpretation. Penelope explains to the beggar that she suffers an inordinate amount of grief, for a god has afflicted her with joyless days and nightmarish sleep (19.513-17). She next asks the beggar to listen to her most recent dream and interpret it:

Twenty geese have I in the house that come out of the water and eat wheat, and my heart warms with joy as I watch them. But down from the mountains there came a great eagle with crooked beak and broke all their necks and killed them; and they lay strewn in a heap in the halls, while he was borne aloft to the bright sky. Now for my part I wept and wailed, in a dream though it was, and round me thronged the fair-tressed Achaean women, as I grieved piteously because the eagle had killed my geese. Then back he came and perched on a projecting roofbeam, and with the voice of a mortal man checked my weeping, and said: "Be of good cheer, daughter of far-famed Icarius; this is no dream, but a true vision of good which, you may be sure, will find fulfillment. The geese are the suitors, and I, that before was the eagle, am now again come back as your husband, who will let loose an ugly doom on all the suitors" *Od.* 19.535-50.

Penelope's dream has generated considerable discussion among classicists. The most difficult aspect of Penelope's dream to explain is the delight which she takes in her geese and her anguish at their slaughter. Some scholars contend that Penelope's love for the geese represents an unconscious affection for her suitors. Anne Vannan Rankin, for example, finds Penelope to be in conflict between fidelity and remarriage and that "it is in this passage which lays bare for us the recesses of Penelope's mind" (1962: 617). Similarly, Joseph Russo writes that the dreaming Penelope is capable of expressing an attitude of desire which is at odds with the waking Penelope's actual faithfulness (1982: 8-11).

Louise Pratt, however, is rightfully skeptical of these Freudian interpretations of unconscious desire, since they are foreign to the ancients under consideration. Pratt instead argues that the geese in Penelope's dream represent Odysseus, and the eagle Zeus (1994: 149). Penelope's grief for her slaughtered geese, then, is an appropriate response for a widow. John Winkler has ingeniously put forward the suggestion that Penelope's entire dream is a fabrication. Winkler argues that Penelope invents the dream in order to test the beggar, whom she suspects to be her husband (1990: 153-9). Penelope does indeed have some reason to suspect that this curious stranger might be her husband - the prophet Theoklymenos has just announced to her that Odysseus is already on the Island (17.157).

The question of Penelope's dream being a ruse need not concern us much in the present study. Whether or not Penelope's dream is real or invented, it is important to note that in 19.535-50 dreams are meaningful expressions of love and longing. At stake in these verses is the truth or falsity of Penelope's undying affection for her husband, and the passage itself addresses issues of her dream's validity. Odysseus informs Penelope that her dream is straight-forward and offers the key its own interpretation: "Lady, in no way is it possible to bend this dream aside and give it another meaning" (*Od.* 19.555). Penelope immediately counters his overconfident claim, expressing a belief that some dreams are true and others false: "'Stranger, know that dreams are baffling and unclear of meaning, and that they do not at all find fulfillment for mankind in every case. For two are the gates of shadowy dreams, and one is fashioned of horn and one of ivory. Those dreams that pass through the gate of sawn ivory deceive men, bringing words that find no fulfillment. But those that come forth through the gate of polished horn bring true things to pass, when any mortal sees them.'"

This passage contains the earliest appearance of a critical attitude towards dreams in Greek literature. Although Penelope opines that in this particular instance her dream probably came from the ivory gate of falsehood (19.563), some dreams are doubtlessly true (19.562). In both the *Iliad* and the *Odyssey*, then, dreams are depicted as potentially valid windows into future events.

Of no small significance is the very fact that it is a dream that serves as the medium for Penelope's desires. Dreams throughout Greco-Roman Antiquity served the function of conveying explicit sexual wishes, which should give pause to readers who insist on her chastity. Let us take two poems from the collection known as the *Greek Anthology* that specify that it is the god Eros who communicates with dreamers, plaguing them with unfulfilled amorous hopes.

In epigram 5.243 a sweet girl acquiesces to the sexual advances of the dreamer, but the jealous god Eros himself wakes the dreamer before intercourse takes place: "I held the laughter-loving girl clasped in my arms in a dream. She yielded herself entirely to me and offered no protest to any of my caprices. But some jealous love lay in ambush for me even at night, and frightening sleep away split my cup of bliss. So even in the dreams of my sleep Eros envies me the sweet attainment of my desire".

Similarly, epigram 12.201 connects Eros with Aphrodite, commanding the "child of the baneful daughter of the foam" to cease his painful dreams of unconsummated love. In contrast, another poet writes that Eros "brought me under my mantle the sweet dream of a softly-laughing boy of eighteen" (*Ep.* 1.125). Another common feature of love-dreams in the *Greek Anthology* is that they are tormenting for the dreamer. After dreams of his favorite boy come to naught, a poet writes: "So sleep, who releases others from toil, brought pain to me, imaging in my soul a loveliness which is living fire" (*Ep.* 2.127).

I believe that scholars have been far too likely to take Penelope's apparent fidelity at face value. As we shall see, however, there are a number of reasons for suspicion on this point. Indeed, through allusions to Helen and Klytaimestra, the text itself foregrounds the ambiguities of Penelope's longings. Most interpreters seem to have been convinced by Agamemnon's vouchsafing for Penelope's fidelity at 24.194-200. It is, however, Homer's choice of this particular witness that should give us pause. Murdered by his own adulterous wife, Klytaimestra, Agamemnon is hardly the best judge on the matter, and it is precisely his witness whose testimony we should question.

Similarly, Athena vouches for Penelope's faithfulness; the deity's own reputation for lying, however, makes her claims suspect in the extreme. Furthermore, Penelope's sympathy for the infamous adulteress Helen (23. 218-24) "leaves the question of Helen's moral responsibility and even the moral status of adultery open and in doubt" (Schein 1995: 25). In sum, the *Odyssey*'s depiction of Penelope's actions, longings, and subjectivity are inherently ambiguous - and exemplary of the many-sided nature of gender and sexuality in the ancient world which the book has discussed.

Appendix One

Male Homoeroticism in the Greco-Roman World

Sexual relations between men were common in ancient Greece. The most popular and celebrated form of Greek male homoeroticism was pederasty (Greek, *paiderastia*, "love for boys"), a complex form of erotic and social interaction between adult men and boys. Pederasty flourished as a social institution directly connected with other social institutions like child rearing and education. Martti Nissinen explains that: "pederastic relationships were seen as an essential part in raising young men to be full-fledged members of society....It was truly a matter of initiation, in which a boy, with the guidance of an adult, would mature into a man in both sexual and social senses" (1998: 58).

Upon maturation a youth was expected to terminate his role as the passive partner and find himself a boy of his own. The relationships were never intended to be between equals: "sexual satisfaction belonged to the active partner [adult], whereas the passive partner [boy] was not allowed to have sexual satisfaction or even aspire to it" (Nissinen 1998: 65). The age difference between the adult men and boys varied, but normally the boy was between twelve and seventeen years old, as seen in the poetry of Strato: "I delight in the prime of a boy of twelve, but one of thirteen is much more desirable. He who is fourteen is a still sweeter flower of the Loves, and one who is just beginning his fifteenth year is yet more delightful. The sixteenth year is that of the gods, and as for the seventeenth it is not for me, but for Zeus, to seek it" (*Greek Anthology* 12.4).

Homoerotic behavior was also common in Rome; "unlike the classical Greeks, the Romans never utilized the homoerotic bond between men to build and sustain their culture but treated homosexuality solely as a source of sexual gratification" (Verstraete 1980: 235). Whereas Greek citizens could engage in pederastic relations in their youth with no social stigma, Romans were more hesitant to penetrate a freeborn citizen. As such, Romans made more frequent use of slaves and prostitutes than did the Greeks.

Although both Greeks and Romans engaged in specific homoerotic practices, one must heavily qualify the statement that "homosexuality was tolerated in Greece and Rome". Both Greeks and Romans constructed a dichotomy between active and passive sexual roles. Michael Satlow explains that "Penetration, which was conceptually linked to status and political power, was the domain of the adult male. The partner penetrated, ideally, was a person of lesser political status, whether a woman, a slave (male or female), or a boy" (1995:1-2). To allow oneself to be penetrated was to open oneself up to charges of effeminacy. Men who desired to be penetrated (Greek *kinaidos*, Latin *cinaedus*) were the targets of constant scorn. If a free man voluntarily submitted himself to the sexual subjugation of another man he identified himself with a woman, slave, prostitute, or foreigner.

Sexual invective and lampoons were used in the political forum to criticize rival opponents. Dionysius of Halicarnassus reports some confusion as to how a former ruler, Aristocrates, earned his nickname "Softie". Some argued that his nickname arose from his gentle nature while others insisted that it originated from Aristocrates allowing himself to be penetrated as a boy. Dionysius writes that the nickname "came to be better known than his own name - either because when a boy he was soft and allowed himself to be treated as a woman, as some relate, or because he was of mild nature and slow to anger, as others state" (*Roman Antiquities* VII 2.4).

Suetonius records in his biographies of the Caesars many accusations of homosexual impropriety being laid against the rulers. The charge that Julius Caesar had been King Nicomedes's catamite was "always a dark stain on his reputation and frequently quoted by his enemies" (*Jul.* 49); the charge was sufficient that the Elder Curio was able to refer to him as "Every woman's husband and every man's wife" (*Jul.* 52). Mark Antony alleged that Julius Caesar made Augustus submit to sexual relations as the price of his adoption (*Aug.* 68) - Augustus easily disproved the accusation by "the decent normality of his sex-life" (*Aug.* 71). Nero was ridiculed for marrying his freed slave and playing the role of the bride: "and on the wedding night he imitated the screams and moans of girl being deflowered" (*Ner.* 29).

Homosexuality in the Jewish Tradition

(a) The Hebrew Bible

In regards to homoeroticism our earliest Jewish writings found in the Hebrew Bible are uniformly negative. In Genesis 19 two of God's angels are dispatched to Sodom to investigate the city's sinfulness. The angels are graciously welcomed by Lot who insists that they spend the night with him (Gen. 19:2). Lot's warm hospitality is contrasted with the violence of the townsfolk, who surround Lot's house and shout: "Where are the men who came to you tonight? Bring them out to us, that we may know them" (Gen.

19:5). Horrified by their demand, Lot offers the crowd his two virgin daughters in lieu of his male guests (Gen. 19:8).

The mob, however, is not interested in Lot's daughters and attempts to break his door down before the two angels strike them with blindness and enable their host's escape (Gen. 19:9-11). The angels then allow Lot some time to gather his family and flee from Sodom before the city is destroyed (Gen. 19:13). God rains down sulfurous fire upon Sodom, which completely annihilates the town and its inhabitants (Gen. 19:24-25). Only Lot and his family are able to escape God's destruction, save for Lot's wife who looks back at the ruined city and is turned into a pillar of salt (Gen. 19:26).

The verb *y'da*) ("to know") clearly has a sexual connotation in verses 5-8; the threat being employed by Lot's people is one of homosexual rape. Derrick Sherwin Bailey's hypothesis that the verb "to know" here lacks a sexual nuance seems unlikely (1955: 3-6); indeed, the narrative quickly becomes nonsensical if the crowd's innocent request to know the credentials of Lot's guests is then countered with the offer of Lot's daughters. The offer of Lot's daughters suggests that a substitution is being made; the threat of homosexual rape is so potent that it is less shaming for a host's family members to be raped than to have his male guests suffer such abuse.

A similar story is recounted in Judges 19-20. A traveling Levite and his concubine are welcomed by a kindly stranger who offers food and shelter (Jud. 19:20). At night a depraved mob surrounds the house and demands "Bring out the man who has come into your house, so that we might know him" (Jud. 19:22). The owner of the house intercedes on his guest's behalf and instead offers the Levite's concubine and his own virgin daughter (Jud. 19:24). When the crowd refuses the concubine is shoved out the door, whereupon she is raped until daybreak (Jud. 19:25).

The narratives of Genesis 19 and Judges 19 are indicative of ancient Israelite views of same-sex rape and male homoeroticism in general. In ancient Israelite culture the act of rape was considered to be a gross infringement on a man's social standing; men who were raped were put into a inferior position usually reserved for women, foreigners, and slaves. In Genesis 19 and Judges 19 the threat of rape is especially wicked in that it is homoerotic: "the homosexual-rape theme is an indicator par excellence of anti-social, malevolent character in ancient Israel" (Niditch 1982: 376).

The Holiness Code: Leviticus 18:22 and 20:13

Two prohibitions against male-male coupling are found in the so-called Holiness Code (Leviticus 17-26), a collection of ancient Israelite legal material. The later of the two laws prescribes the death penalty for both of the guilty parties involved:

> Do not lie with a male as one lies with a woman; it is an abhorrence (Lev. 18:22)
> If a man lies with a male as one lies with a woman, the two of them have done an abhorrent thing; they shall be put to death - their bloodguilt is upon them (Lev. 20:13)

Leviticus 18 and 20 are quite similar in scope and content. The prohibitions against male same-sex practices are found amidst various incest taboos (18:7-16; 20:11-12) and laws concerned with bestiality (18:23; 20:15), adultery (18:20; 20:10), and sexual relations with menstruating women (18:19; 20:18). Both chapters outline proper sexual behavior and caution the Israelites not to follow the examples of their wayward Egyptian and Canaanite neighbors (18:3, 20:23). Sexual acts between males are described as a *toeivah*, "an abhorrence." The term was often used to describe acts that were thought to be characteristic of the Egyptians and the Canaanites, including unclean foods and taboo sexual relations.

The language used in the Levitical prohibitions sheds some light on their exact meaning. Saul Olyan has convincingly argued that Leviticus 18:22 and 20:13 specifically forbade male-male anal intercourse, not male same-sex practices in general. Olyan writes that the laws "seem to refer specifically to intercourse and suggest that anal penetration was seen as analogous to vaginal penetration on some level, since 'the lying down of a woman' seems to mean vaginal receptivity" (1998: 400. To be penetrated was to take on a female role; this unmanly act confused the very boundaries, distinctions, and categories that the authors of the Holiness Code went to great lengths to establish.

(B) APOCRYPHA AND PSEUDEPIGRAPHA

The Apocrypha and Pseudepigrapha to which the Sibylline Oracles belong are non-canonical Jewish writings from approximately 200 B.C.E. - 100 C.E. which help to illuminate aspects of Judaism in the Hellenistic world. The Apocrypha and Pseudepigrapha make frequent reference to homosexual relations, usually in conjunction with the depravity of the Gentiles. Sodom is often mentioned as the symbol of a perverted lifestyle (see, for example, *Jubilees* 13:17; 16:5-6; 22:22). Whereas Old and New Testament references to Sodom emphasize the Sodomite's avarice and insensitivity to the poor (Isa. 1:10, Jer. 23:14, and Ezek. 16:49), Apocryphal and Pseudepigraphal writings show clear sexual nuances in the sin of Sodom.

It is difficult to ascertain the extent to which homoeroticism is connoted in these references. Only *2 Enoch* 10:4-5 explicitly mentions the sin of Sodom as homoerotic. Here the reference is to pederasty: "This place, Enoch, has been prepared for those who do not glorify God, who practice on the earth the sin which is against nature, which is child corruption in the anus in the manner of Sodom." Other descriptions of the Sodomite's sexual sins are ambiguous and homoeroticism has to be read between the lines (*Jubilees* 20:5, *Testament of Levi* 14:6-7, *Testament of Benjamin* 9.1).

Denouncements of homoeroticism also occur outside of reference to the city of Sodom. *The Testament of Levi* includes pederasts in a list of sinners: "In the seventh week there will come priests: idolators, adulterers, money lovers, arrogant, lawless, voluptuaries, pederasts, those who practice bestiality" (17:11). The *Sentences of Pseudo-Phocylides* condemns male homoeroticism more generally. Here the argument advanced is that same-sex practices are so degenerate that even animals will not partake in them: "Do not transgress with unlawful sex the limits set by nature. For even animals are not pleased by intercourse of male with male" (vv. 190-191). A final reference to homoeroticism found in the *Letter of Aristeas* likens male prostitution to incest: "The majority of other men defile themselves in their relationships, thereby committing a serious offense, and lands and whole cities take pride in it: they not only procure the males, they also defile mothers and daughters" (152).

(C) Rabbinic texts

Rabbinic texts occasionally refer to same-sex practices, habitually describing them as Gentile vices. Particularly interesting is *Qiddushin* 5:10, which explicitly states that Israel is not suspected of this sin. In keeping with their Hellenistic background, these discussions are almost invariably concerned with pederastic relationships. *Sanhedrin* 7.4 recommends that homosexual behavior is to be punished by stoning - minors are not considered culpable. Sexual relations between men and youths are read in a few surprising places in Midrash. Potiphar, for instance, is said to have taken an erotic interest in the young Joseph (*Sotah* 13b) and Ham is accused of sexually violating his father Noah (*Sanhedrin* 70a).

(D) Philo of Alexandria and Josephus

The voluminous writings of Philo of Alexandria and Josephus provide us with invaluable information regarding first Century Judaism. Josephus and Philo both interpret the story of Sodom as a warning against pederasty (*On Abraham* 135-136, *Jewish Antiquities* 1.194-204). Both authors also make use of the natural sex argument and describe same-sex practices as habits which corrupt one's soul. Josephus describes homoerotic behavior as a Gentile vice when discussing the superiority of Jewish Law: "The Law recognizes no sexual connections, except for the natural union of man and wife, and that only for procreation of children. Sodomy it abhors, and punishes any guilty of such assault with death" (*Against Apion* 2.199).

Philo so describes the people of Sodom: "Not only in their mad lust for women did they violate the marriages of their neighbors, but also men mounted males without respect for the sex nature which the active partner shares with the passive....not only did they emasculate their bodies by softness and voluptuousness but they worked a further degeneration in their souls" (*On Abraham* 135-136). For Philo homosexual behavior was part of a degenerating process which confounds the natural gender boundaries and alienates one from God. What most bothers Philo is the degree to which same-sex relations are openly flaunted:

"Much graver than the above is another evil, which has ramped its way into the cities, namely pederasty. In former days the very mention of it was a great disgrace, but now it is a matter of boasting not only to the active but to the passive partners, who habituate themselves to endure the disease of effemination, let both body and soul run to waste, and leave no ember of their male sex-nature to smoulder" (*The Special Laws* 3.37).

Appendix Two

Further References to Jews in Roman Satire

Primary Sources

JUVENAL (*CA.* 60 - *CA.* 130 CE) describes how the barbarian Agrippa gave his sister a famous diamond ring to commemorate their incestuous union. This event took place in a land where it's inhabitants abstained from eating pork: "It [the diamond] was given as a present long ago by the barbarian Agrippa to his incestuous sister, in that country where kings celebrate festal Sabbaths with bare feet, and where a long-established clemency suffers pigs to attain old age" (*Satires* 6.156-160). In this account the Jews do not abstain from pork because of religious convictions. Instead they seem to refuse to eat pork because they feel merciful toward pigs. Juvenal's fanciful addition of kings celebrating the Sabbath with bare feet was probably included to make the Sabbath seem decidedly ludicrous.

Petronius also mentions Jewish abhorrence of pork. He does so in a manner that might impart a theological significance to the custom: "The Jew may worship his pig-god and clamour in the ears of high heaven, but unless he cuts back his foreskin with the knife, he shall go forth from the people and emigrate to Greek cities, and shall not tremble at the fasts of Sabbath imposed by the law" (*Fragment* 37). Although Petronius' curious description of the Jews worshiping a pig-god could perhaps be an attempt to rationally explain why the Jews refrained from eating pork, the reference could just has easily been added simply to ridicule the Jews.

Jewish poverty is one of the most striking themes in Latin satire. Although Roman Jews occasionally acquired wealth, most were illiterate laborers or low-ranking craftsmen; satirists made extensive use of this lack of wealth. Persius (*ca.* 34-62 CE) describes the cheap entertainments of the Sabbath: "But when the day of Herod comes round, when the lamps wreathed with violets and ranged round the greasy window-sills have spat forth their thick clouds of smoke, when the floppy tunnies' tails are curled round the dishes of red ware, and the white jars are swollen out with wine, you silently twitch your lips, turning pale at the Sabbath of the circumcised" (*Satires* 5.179-84). The poem is filled with signs of Jewish poverty. The Jews dine off of common red earthenware dishes and consume the tail, the coarsest part of the fish.

Juvenal depicts the Jews as poverty-stricken beggars who frequent a once-sacred grove associated with the pious King Numa Pompilius: "Here Numa held his nightly assignations with his mistress; but now the holy fount and grove and shrine are let out to Jews, who possess a basket and a truss of hay for all of their belongings. For as every tree nowadays has to pay toll to the people, the Muses have been ejected, and the wood has to go a-begging" (*Satires* 3.12-

16). Juvenal elsewhere speaks of a begging Jewess who interprets dreams for a pittance (6.542-47) and a Roman beggar who haunts a synagogue with poor Jewish companions (3.296). Martial (*ca.* 40-104 CE) retreats to his country estate to escape from Jews taught by their mothers to beg.

Although Sabbath leisure was frequently mentioned, no author displays much knowledge of the subject. In his fourth epigram Martial insults a certain Bassa, a woman of questionable morals whom he loathes: "The stench of the bed of a drained march; of the raw vapours of sulphur springs; the putrid reek of a sea-water fishpond; of a stale he-goat in the midst of his amours; of the breath of fasting Sabbatarian women... - all these stenches would I prefer to your stench, Bassa!" (*Epigrams* 4.4). Bassa's stench is more offensive than the breath of women fasting on the Sabbath, a possible effect of halitosis.

Martial recognized Sabbath leisure as a Jewish practice but mistakenly believed the day to be one of fasting; Horace (65-8 BCE) too betrays a similar ignorance of the Sabbath. When pestered by a man he dislikes, Horace spots his friend Fuscus Aristius passing by. Hoping to be saved, Horace calls out to his friend: "'Surely you said there was something you wanted to tell me in private." Fuscus replies, "'I mind it well, but I'll tell you at a better time. Today is the thirtieth day, a Sabbath. Would you affront the circumcised Jews?'" The meaning of the "thirtieth day" has generated considerable discussion among scholars. It ultimately remains uncertain why Horace mentions the thirtieth day in connection with the Sabbath, but seems most likely that the reference merely reflects the author's ignorance of the Sabbath and the Jewish calendar. What is more certain is that Horace is mocking a pagan friend for partaking in Jewish custom.

Lastly, Juvenal speaks of Sabbath leisure with great disdain. He bitterly describes Jews who "gave up every seventh day to idleness, keeping it apart from all the concerns of life." These sentiments formed part of a longstanding tradition that regarded the Sabbath as an excuse to shirk duties.

APPENDIX THREE

THE CONTRIBUTION OF MEDICAL ANTHROPOLOGY

FOR THOSE UNFAMILIAR WITH THE emerging field of Medical Anthropology and sufficiently interested in contextualizing women and illness in Antiquity, this appendix offers a brief overview of the ways in which the social history of medicine is undergoing a time of complete reassessment. Beginning in the 1970's, and largely in part stimulated by the emergence of postmodernist studies and the work of Michel Foucault and Clifford Geertz, cultural approaches to medicine have since been thoroughly reconceptualized towards an understanding of illness, disease, and their "treatment" as socially-determined discourses, social institutions, and frameworks for viewing the larger world. The impact of postmodernist tools of deconstruction, defamiliariztion, and decenterdness has been enormous; virtually all studies in the social history of medicine currently being produced are set within the frame of postmodernism

(Singer 1990: 290-91). As the postmodern project has called into question the value of universalizing formulations, scholars have lost faith in the ability of contemporary Western constructions of health and illness to provide the framework for viewing health and sickness in disparate cultures. In this regard, the postmodernist analyses of Foucault have undoubtedly had the greatest impact in reshaping medical anthropology.

In his much-celebrated study on the emergence of modern hospitals, penitentiaries, and asylums, Foucault examined the institutionalization of clinical medicine while working under the premise that illness and its treatment were socially-constructed phenomena (1973). By utilizing his own concept of discourse as a hegemonic, meaning-making force that under specific historical circumstances defines and delimits objects of representation, Foucault persuasively argued that the present-day Western conceptions of health and wellness were cultural products devoid of any inherent stability that could indeed be traced to a series of very specific processes starting in the 18th century. Contemporaneously with Foucault, Clifford Geertz reshaped the field of Anthropology with his much-reprinted 1973 essay "'From the Native's Point of View': On the Nature of Anthropological Understanding," a landmark study that provided a critical investigation into the concepts of "experience-near" and "experience-distant" approaches to data in Anthropological inquiry.

In the decades following Foucault, Geertz, and further studies, the field of medical anthropology has become better attuned to the culturally-specific frameworks for conceptualizing, experiencing, and treating illness. I take as representative of this fact Merrill Singer's assertion that "exploring the contestable nature of culture provides a route for understanding the role of power and social struggle in shaping various features of the health domain, including the 'identification' of disease, the practice patterns of providers, and the popularity of treatments, that are assumed to be dictated by science rather than created by culture" (1990: 298). Alongside this new attenuation to illness as a cultural construct is a growing awareness of the impact of historic factors, political structures, and economic realities on actual lived experiences of illness as well as an appreciation of the ways in which health and disease are experienced at both the individual and collective levels.

In this regard, Marxist analysis and Foucault's understanding of hegemonic discourse have proved themselves to be particularly well-suited for bringing to light the enormous roles that political and economic structures play in various health systems. At the macro-level, societal beliefs regarding the sick or infirm individuals' (diminished) honor, status, and treatment in society, medical discourse directly supports constructions that often (though not invariably) negatively impact the sick while affirming the powerful normalcy of the temporarily-abled. At the micro-level, it follows that in non-egalitarian societies with unequal distributions of wealth and property individuals will have wildly divergent nutrients, housing/shelter, and access to institutionalized medical treatments and their accompanying benefits. Class differentials, then, in methods of treatment and in prevalence of certain kinds of illness feature prominently in any medical context.

As medical discourse is part and parcel of hegemonic ideology, it thus both builds up and capitulates with structures of oppression and (mis) appropriations of power: "medical practice or any practice imbued with the meanings and logics of the worlds that human beings construct, practice that is directed immediately to the body, carries hegemonic possibility tot he very heart of lived reality" (Kapferer 1988:432). In various times and places (including, I will argue, the ancient Mediterranean), the medical system and its constructs have directly contributed to structures of domination. As well shall soon see, an understanding of the medical system proves itself to be invaluable in bringing to light pervasive ideologies, social conflict, and the exercise of power over women in the classical Antiquity.

Before proceeding with our examination of medicine in the Greco-Roman world, however, let us first clarify our terms and make explicit what is meant by conceptions of "illness," "disease," etc. Although it might seem pedantic, a working understanding of the language of medicine (both ancient and modern) is imperative if one is to avoid grossly anachronistic interpretations of our ancient texts. As best formulated by M.D. Grmek:

> It is impossible to apprehend correctly the significance of an ancient text concerning a pathological event unless we rid ourselves as completely as possible of the ontological notion of disease embedded in our everyday language. Notions of disease and even of particular diseases do not flow from our experiences. They are explanatory models of reality, not its constitutive elements. To put it simply, diseases exist only in the realm of ideas. They interpret a complex empirical reality and presuppose a certain medical philosophy or pathological system of reference (1989: 1).

To aid in this regard, the present study will employ emic terminology whenever possible and organic, as opposed to modern frameworks and diagnoses that are at best ahistoric and at worst tendentious and damaging. Nevertheless, *some* language of health and illness is of course necessary, however diligently one might endeavor to read the medical lexicon in its cultural context. What follows is a brief attempt to clarify our terms.

"Health" is perhaps our most ephemeral term. In common parlance the word most often denotes a broad frame of reference to describe an individual's well-being as defined by their particular culture. Health often - though not necessarily - refers to physical, mental, and social well-being. Since, however, the Cartesian dichotomies of body/mind, spirit/body are inapplicable or perhaps more accurately inadequate in regards to the Ancients, health might best understood as an individual's social well-being. One can easily see how quickly "health" can slide into "normalcy", - "a state in which the person is performing to his own and other's satisfaction the roles appropriate to his situation in society" (Wallace 2003: 247-48). While health in Antiquity is profoundly related to societal expectations, as the term "normalcy" often connotes Western and Capitalist notions of self-sufficiency, "health" is to be preferred.

The distinction between "disease" and "illness" is similarly ambiguous. Essentially, illness encompasses more than disease. Disease is the more specific of the two terms and is most properly used to describe a singular, very exact impairment of human organs. The present study will take up Anthony Wallace's proposal that the following categories might better represent diverse cultures than do Western diagnostic categories: mild versus severe, and intermittent versus continuous (1988: 253). Mildness and severity refer to the degree of abnormality of the overt behavior itself (note the emphasis on overt behavior [read: observable to society] as opposed to internalized processes which may have little or no effect on a person's social conditions and standing).

Intermittent and continuous refer to a disease's frequency of occurrence, with intermittence describing "discrete attacks separated by intervals of normalcy, and continuousness as the half in which the disorder can be characterized as a period of uninterrupted dysfunction" (Wallace 1988: 253). Less stigma accompanies intermittent diseases, as they are perceived as only occasionally impairing an individual's ability to carry out their socially-prescribed function. Continuous diseases are also far more likely to incur harsh (my value judgment) treatments of confinement, banishment, execution, or invasive medical procedures.

And, finally: "curing" most properly describes the attempt to effect a given disease- a singular specific abnormality- while the term "healing" best describes a broader effort "to provide personal and social meaning for the life problems created by sickness." Curing is sometimes synonymous with "treatment" - an effort to improve, tolerate, or make best use of the victim. The treatment or cure of an individual (which aims at re-integrating said individual back into society) is to be differentiated from extrusion - the previously mentioned and all-too common responses of confinement, banishment, or execution - which seeks to effect positive change in society as opposed to the individual. When seen alongside treatment/curing, "healing" has far wider cultural implications.

The medical schematization of illness and healing is a meaning-imbued constellation of beliefs and practices. One of the primary functions of healing is to make sense of the individual and social experience of illness. As the individual is healed, community-formation is reinforced as she is integrated back into solidarity with her larger community: "The healing dialectic has been considered effective when the bonds between the sick individual and the group, weakened by disease, are strengthened, social values reaffirmed, and the notion of social order no longer threatened" (Kleinman 1973: 210). Reintegration into society signifies the triumph and efficacy of social order, the validity of the culture's worldview. *Cosmic dramas of death and renewal, fecundity and scarcity, of life itself are physically embodied and signified in the healing process.* Healing extends then far beyond surface-level physiological processes to include the very beliefs, values, and feelings of the cultural system.

BIBLIOGRAPHY

Adler, Elaine. The Background for the Metaphor of Covenant as Marriage in the Hebrew Bible. Unpublished Ph.D. dissertation. University of California, Berkeley, 1989.

Alter, Robert. The Art of Biblical Narrative. New York: Basic Books, 1981.

Barré, Michael. "The Meaning of prsdn in Judges III 22" Vetus Testamentum 41 (1991): 229-45.

Barthes, Roland. Mythologies. New York: Hill and Wang, 1972.

Bird, Phyllis. "To Play the Harlot: An Inquiry into an Old Testament

Metaphor." in Gender and Difference in Ancient Israel, ed. Peggy Day. Minneapolis: Fortress Press, 1989: 75-94.

Boswell, John. Christianity, Social Tolerance, and Homosexuality: Gay People in Western Europe from the Beginning of the Christian Era to the Fourteenth Century. Chicago: University of Chicago Press, 1980.

Bowra, C.M. Greek Lyric Poetry. Oxford University Press, 1962.

Brock, Roger. "Sickness in the Body Politic: medical imagery in the Greek polis" in Death and Disease in the Ancient City, ed. Valerie M. Hope and Eireann Marshall, London: Routledge, 2000: 24-34.

Carson, Anne. "Putting Her in Her Place: Women, Dirt, and Desire" in Before Sexuality: The Construction of Erotic Experience in the Ancient Greek World, ed. David M. Halperin, John J. Winkler, and Froma I. Zeitlin, Princeton University Press, 1990: 135-169.

Charlesworth, James, ed. The Old Testament Pseudepigrapha. Garden City: Doubleday, 1983.

Cohen, Shaye J.D. "Did Martial Have a Circumcised Jewish Slave?," in The

Jews in the Hellenistic-Roman World, edited by Isaiah M. Gafni, Aharon Oppenheimer, Daniel R. Schwartz (Jerusalem: The Historical Society of Israel, 1996).

Countryman, William. Dirt, Greed, and Sex: Sexual Ethics in the New Testament and Their Implication for Today. Philadelphia: Fortress Press, 1988.

David, R. "Rationality versus Irrationality" in Egyptian Medicine in the Pharaonic and Graeco-Roman Periods, in Magic and Rationality in the Ancient Near East, ed. R. David: 127-39.

Day, Linda. "Rhetoric and Domestic Violence in Ezekiel 16." Biblical Interpretation 8:3 (2000): 205-230.

Day, Peggy. "Adulterous Jerusalem's Imagined Desire.": Vetus Testamentum 50 (2000): 285-309.

"The Bitch Had it Coming to Her: Rhetoric and Interpretation in Ezekiel 16." Biblical Interpretation 8:3 (2000): 231-254.

De Young, James. "A Critique of Prohomosexual Interpretations of the Old Testament Apocrypha and Pseudepigrapha." Bibliotheca Sacra 157 (1990): 437-454.

Dean-Jones, Lesley. Women's Bodies in Classical Greek Science, Oxford: Clarendon Press, 1994.

Devereux, George "The Nature of Sappho's Seizure in fr. 31 LP as Evidence of Her Inversion" Classical Quarterly 1967: 17-31.

Eco, Umberto.

1979. The Role of the Reader: Explorations in the Semiotics of Texts. Bloomington: Indiana University Press.

1984. Semiotics and the Philosophy of Language. Bloomington: Indiana University Press.

1990. The Limits of Interpretation. Bloomington: Indiana University Press.

Exum, J. Cheryl. Plotted, Shot, and Painted: Cultural Representations of Biblical Women. Journal for the Study of the Old Testament Supplement Series 215. Sheffield: Sheffield Academic Press, 1996.

Foucault, Michel. The Birth of the Clinic: An Archaeology of Medical Perception. New York: Vintage Books, 1973.

Geertz, Clifford. The Interpretation of Cultures. New York: Basic Books, 1973.

Geffcken, J. Die Oracula Sibyllina. Griechischen Christlichen Schriftseller: Leipzig, 1902.

Gilula, Dwora "Did Martial Have a Jewish Slave? (7.35)." Classical Quarterly 37 (1987): 531-2.

Harris, William. Sappho: The Greek Poems. Middlebury College, privately published, n.d.

Highet, Gilbert. Juvenal the Satirist. Oxford: Clarendon Press, 1962.

Jackson, Ralph. Doctors and Diseases in the Roman Empire, Norman: University of Oklahoma Press, 1988.

Kamionkowski, S. Tamar. Gender Reversal and Cosmic Chaos. Sheffield: Sheffield Academic Press, 2003.

Kapferer, B. "Gramsci's Body and a Critical Medical Anthropology" <u>Medical Anthropological Quarterly 2</u> (1988): 426-432.

King, Helen. <u>Hippocrates' Woman: Reading the Female Body in Ancient Greece</u>, Routledge: London, 1998.

Kleinman, Arthur. "Medicine's Symbolic Reality: On a Central Problem in the Philosophy of Medicine" <u>Inquiry</u> 16 (1973): 206-13.

Koch, Timothy R. "Cruising as Methodology" in <u>Queer Commentary and the Hebrew Bible</u>, ed. Ken Stone. Sheffield: Sheffield Academic Press, 2001.

Lefkowitz, Mary. "Critical Stereotypes and the Poetry of Sappho" in <u>Reading Sappho</u>, ed. Ellen Greene. Berkeley: University of California Press, 1996: 26-34.

Maines, Rachel. The Technology of Orgasm. John Hopkins University Press, 1999.

Malti-Douglas, Fedwa. <u>The Starr Report Disrobed</u>. New York: Columbia University Press, 2000.

Martin, Dale. "Arsenokoitês and Malakos: Meanings and Consequences" in Biblical Ethics & Homosexuality: Listening to Scripture, ed. Robert Brawley. Louisville: Westminster John Knox Press, 1996.

Miles, Johnny E. Wise King - Royal Fool: Semiotics, Satire, and Proverbs 1-9 JSOT Sup Series 399. London: T & T Clark, 2005.

Mobley, Gregory. The Empty Men: The Heroic Tradition of Ancient Israel. New York: Doubleday, 2005.

Nelson, Dana D. and Tyler Curtain "The Symbolics of Presidentialism: Sex and Democratic Identification" in Our Monica, Ourselves, ed. Lauren Berlant and Lisa Duggan. New York University Press, 2001: 34-54.

Nissinen, Martti. Homoeroticism in the Biblical World: A Historical Perspective. Minneapolis: Fortress Press, 1998.

Norton, Kevin I. et. al. "Ken and Barbie at Life Size." Sex Roles 34: 287-94.

Nutton, Vivian. "Medicine in the Greek World: 800-50 BC" in The Western Medical Tradition, ed. Lawrence I. Conrad et. al. Cambridge Unviersity Press, 1995: 11-38.

Olyan, Saul. "'And With a Male You Shall Not Lie the Lying Down of a Woman': On the Meaning and Significance of Leviticus 18:22 and 20:13" Journal of the History of Sexuality 5 (1994): 179-206.

Page, Denys. Sappho and Alcaeus. Oxford: Clarendon Press, 1955.

Quirke, Stephen. "Reading Gender in Ancient Egyptian Healing Papyri" in National Healths, ed. Michael Worton, UCL Press, 2004: 173-86.

Rand, Erica. Barbie's Queer Accessories. Durham: Duke University Press, 1995.

Schein, Seth L. "Female Representations and Interpreting the Odyssey" in The Distaff Side, ed. Beth Cohen. Oxford University Press, 1995: 17-28.

Schneider, Cy. Children's Television. Lincolnwood: NTC Business, 1987.

Setel, T. Dorah. "Prophets and Pornography: Female Sexual Imagery in Hosea." in Feminist Interpretation of the Bible, ed. Letty M. Russell. Philadelphia: Westminster Press, 1985: 86-95.

Shields, Mary. "Multiple Exposures: Body Rhetoric and Gender

Characterization in Ezekiel 16." Journal of Feminist Studies in Religion 14 (1998): 5-18.

Singer, Merrill. "Postmodernism and Medical Anthropology: Words of Caution" Medical Anthropology 12 (1990): 289-304.

Snyder, Jane McIntosh. Lesbian Desire in the Lyrics of Sappho. New York: Columbia University Press, 1997.

St. John, Maria "How to Do Things with the Starr Report: Pornography, Performance, and the President's Penis" in Porn Studies, ed. Linda Williams. Durham: Duke University Press, 2004.

Thomas, Jeannie Banks. Naked Barbies, Warrior Joes, and Other Forms of Visible Gender. Chicago: University of Illinois Press, 2003.

Torres, Sasha "Sex of a Kind: On Graphic Language and the Modesty of Television News" in Our Monica, Ourselves, ed. Lauren Berlant and Lisa Duggan. New York University Press, 2001: 102-115.

Torrey, Charles. The Apocryphal Literature. New Haven: Yale University Press, 1945.

Wallace, Anthony FC. "Mental Illness, Biology, and Culture" in Revitalizations and Mazeways, ed. Robert S. Grant. Lincoln: University of Nebraska Press (2003): 225-261.

Witke, Charles. Latin Satire: The Structure of Persuasion (Leiden: E.J. Brill, 1970).

Winkler, Jack. "Gardens of Nymphs: Private and Public in Sappho's Lyrics" in Reading Sappho, ed. Ellen Greene. Berkeley: University of California Press, 1996: 89-112.

Wood, Dennis and John Fels "Designs on Signs" Cartographica 23 (1986): 54-104.

Wright, David. "Homosexuals or Prostitutes? The Meaning of ARSENOKOITAI (1Cor. 6:9, 1 Tim. 1:10)" Vigiliae Christianae 38 (1984).